SHADES OF DANIEL BOONE

A Personal View of Special Ops and the War in Vietnam

CSM Walter J. Jackson
USA (Ret)

HERITAGE BOOKS
2014

HERITAGE BOOKS
AN IMPRINT OF HERITAGE BOOKS, INC.

Books, CDs, and more—Worldwide

For our listing of thousands of titles see our website
at
www.HeritageBooks.com

Published 2014 by
HERITAGE BOOKS, INC.
Publishing Division
5810 Ruatan Street
Berwyn Heights, Md. 20740

Copyright © 2005 Walter J. Jackson

All rights reserved. No part of this book may be reproduced or transmitted in any form or by any means, electronic or mechanical, including photocopying, recording or by any information storage and retrieval system without written permission from the author, except for the inclusion of brief quotations in a review.

International Standard Book Numbers
Paperbound: 978-0-7884-3228-6
Clothbound: 978-0-7884-6012-8

This book is dedicated to all the service men and women who served honorably in Vietnam, to my brothers Bill, Norman, and Alan who also served, and especially to Col. Edward Skender, USA (Ret.), who helped me greatly by editing and providing comments and motivation.

CONTENTS

Introduction vii

1 THE REASON FOR BEING, THE OBSTACLES,
   AND THE RISKS 1

2 THE MISSIONS
   AND THE RULES OF ENGAGEMENT 9

3 HOW THE OPERATIONS WERE CONDUCTED 13

4 THE SOLDIERS 31

5 WEAPONS, EQUIPMENT, AND SUPPLIES 35

6 SUPPORT 43

7 LIVING CONDITIONS 49

8 INSERTIONS 57

9 EXTRACTIONS 61

10 THE MIND AND BODY ADAPTS 65

11 A DAY OF REALIZATION 67

12 PLANS CHANGE WITH THE FIRST SHOT 71

13 AN ENEMY ATTACK 77

14 SOME NOT SO BRIGHT IDEAS 83

15 THE ENEMY CAN BE STUPID TOO 89

16 STRANGERS IN THE WOODS 93

17 HOW CLOSE CAN YOU GET 99

18 THE LLDB 105

19 WHAT I REMEMBER 109

20	WOMEN AND BABY KILLERS	119
21	WHAT WENT WRONG	123
22	SHOULD WE HAVE BEEN THERE	131
23	WAS IT WORTH IT	135
24	A QUICK HISTORY LESSON	137
Glossary		147
Bibliography		153

INTRODUCTION

It has been thirty-six years since I walked the dusty trails in the central highlands of Vietnam. Over the years, the questions of "What was it like" and "What did you do there" were often put off with a quick answer that was really a quiet refusal to talk about those days of a youth long past.

Project Delta, Sigma, and Omega were the original designations for the operations that sent reconnaissance teams across the border of South Vietnam into Laos, North Vietnam, southern China and Cambodia. By the time I arrived in country, the short but adventurous expeditions westward into Cambodia had been renamed Daniel Boone. The operations into Laos were conducted under the name of Shining Brass and then Prairie Fire. The operations into Cambodia would again be renamed Salem House before they were ended in 1972.

A couple of hundred years ago, Daniel Boone went west on several occasions. He went into what is now Kentucky in search of new lands and opportunities for his family and others. Like Daniel on his reconnaissance missions, our teams went west in search of opportunities. The opportunities were not the type of opportunities that old Daniel was looking for. But they were opportunities just the same.

Like Daniel, we had to worry with figuring out which of the natives were hostile and which were not. We both went and explored areas patrolled by superior hostile forces. The vegetation we encountered was different, but the terrain was similar. We both risked death in doing what we wanted to do. Daniel bragged about where he had gone and what he had seen in an effort to recruit new settlers. We, the soldiers in special operations, could not do that for many years. Now that those operations have been declassified, it is the time for some of us to talk about what we saw and what we did in those days long ago. This is my attempt to do so.

Was what we did important? The President was briefed daily on the operations and the intelligence that was gathered by Studies and Observation Group operations. I was told in my initial briefings at Command and Control South that the President was involved to the extent of approving and rejecting some of them. That in itself is a pretty strong indicator of the importance of what we did there.

This book is about what I saw and experienced as a member of B-50, SOA, 5th Special Forces Group during the mid- to late 1960s. It is an effort to answer the many questions I have been asked; questions such as: what was it like, what did you do there, how did you do it, did you ever kill anybody, does the war in Vietnam still affect you, how close did you ever come to being killed, don't you think it was all a waste, and did you like being there? It is my story. It is my view of the Vietnam War. It is also the story of Special Forces and Special Ops in Vietnam.

SOG/CCS Plaque Emblem

1

REASON FOR BEING
THE OBSTACLES AND THE RISKS

When I was a trainee in Special Forces Training Group, an old veteran of War II, Korea, and Vietnam told me the following. It was his story of why we were in Vietnam. He said that Ho Chi Minh worked with the US government and the OSS (Office of Strategic Services) during our war with Japan. After WWII and before Vietnam was divided into North and South Vietnam, Ho Chi Minh, told the US government that he was a communist but embraced many of the principles and ideals that made the US a great country. He wanted to be a friend of America and trade with us. But, he wanted to kick the French out of his country. Our government told him to go screw himself; that we didn't deal with communists. Basically the United States became involved in Vietnam because of a policy of containment in regards to the growth of communism, any form of communism, and because we were allied with France.

Project Delta, the mother of special operations in Vietnam, was established in 1964 to do long range patrolling and gather intelligence. Delta personnel became a source for the other special operations programs that followed. Experienced Delta team members became instructors in a school that trained others in the skills required to conduct long range patrolling in the rain forests of Vietnam. The organization to which I was assigned was established to gather information that could be used to stop the flow of men and materials that were moving from North Vietnam through Cambodia to South Vietnam.

The Truong Son Route (Vietnamese for Long Mountains Route and more widely known as the Ho Chi Minh Trail) was used by North Vietnam to infiltrate soldiers and supplies into South Vietnam. The birth of the trails began in WWII with the use of footpaths used by the Viet Minh to fight the Japanese. They were improved during 1946 through 1954 in the Viet Minh's war against French colonialism. Enlargement and improvements were made during the North's war with South Vietnam and the United States forces.

Starting near Vinh, in mountain passes in North Vietnam, the trail crossed into Laos, ran south through Cambodia, and ended with trails into South Vietnam. The most southerly end reached Tay Ninh Province on the edge of the Mekong Delta. The trail was a wide network of footpaths, cart tracks, and roads. In addition to these high and low speed pathways, there were rest camps, assembly areas, base camps, training areas, equipment caches, truck parks, repair facilities, guard posts, guide posts, and anti aircraft batteries. Over three hundred thousand workers maintained the ten thousand miles of roads and trails. These workers consisted of North Vietnamese and local forced labor conscripts. Because of the difficult terrain, a soldier walking from the start of the trail to Mekong Delta required a travel time of five to six months.

In 1966, intelligence estimates indicated four to five thousand North Vietnamese personnel and thirty to fifty tons of supplies were being moved south over the trail each year. This was based on an estimate of three and a half to four tons in military supplies and four to five hundred reinforcements coming south each month. A way had to be found to stop this infiltration. The 1962 Geneva Accords made Cambodia a neutral country. The Peoples Army of Vietnam, the NVA, ignored the accords. Our government did not. Conventional combat units could not be used. So a plan was devised to use covert special operations personnel and air power to stem the flood of troops and war materials moving south.

For operations in Cambodia, a secret deal was made with its government. The US was granted permission to covertly enter Cambodia up to a maximum depth of thirty kilometers. The operations had to be covert to prevent greater problems and deepening the conflict between Cambodia and North Vietnam. Cambodia had a small and ill equipped army and was no match for the North Vietnamese forces already operating along the Cambodian border.

The plan for stopping the flow of men and materials through Laos and Cambodia was simple. Special ops personnel would perform reconnaissance missions and locate targets suitable for attack by air assets. The air assets included fighter bombers, gunships, and saturation bombing by B-52's (Arc lights). In addition they would monitor the flow of men and material to assess the effectiveness of the air campaign and perform other missions as the command deemed necessary. Because of the secret deal with the government of Cambodia and the restriction of US forces operating there, the President of the United States had to deny the use of military personnel and the military actions taking place there.

The obstacles to accomplishing the missions consisted of the following:

1. NVA soldiers and support personnel in and around the trail networks. The NVA soldiers moving south moved in groups. The size of the groups varied in number. In addition to the hundreds of soldiers that were moving south on the trail, support personnel were assigned along sections of the trail to man antiaircraft weapons, operate a communications network, operate rest areas, gather food stuffs and operate feeding areas, repair damage done through bombing, and recruit or force locals to work on the trail networks.

2. The placement of guards and guide personnel at trail junctions and on clearings large enough to be used as an LZ. Guides were stationed along the trail to guide the troops moving south. One guide would take a group to the end of his area where the next guide would take over. Then the first guide would return to guide the next group. Guards were posted in

areas of high activity to watch for intruders and collect or capture shot down pilots.

3. Trained and dedicated trackers were stationed along the trail to pick up the trail of intruders. Soldiers and local people skilled in tracking were used to track and find intruders.

4. The placement of mines and booby traps at locations most likely to be used by intruders. Areas that had been used before by US personnel were often mined or booby trapped.

5. The monitoring of radio frequencies used by US forces. The NVA monitored the radio frequencies found on standard American military radios.

6. The indigenous people living in and moving about in the area. There was no way to tell the local friendly people from those who worked for or with the NVA. We therefore treated everyone the same.

7. The VC spy network inside South Vietnam. There was an extensive spy network working in South Vietnam. Most of the US camps had spies employed inside them or spies that lived nearby.

8. The excellent camouflage techniques and discipline of the NVA. The NVA and VC were very conscience of the need for good camouflage. Failure to maintain good camouflage usually resulted in bombs dropping from the sky.

9. The fact that a lot of facilities were underground. Many of the facilities like hospitals, supply caches, and rest areas were underground. The NVA and VC dug miles and miles of tunnels inside South Vietnam and along the trail network. They also made use of natural caves.

10. The heavy use of the trail taking place during the hours of darkness. Most of the movement along the trail took place from dusk to just past dawn. Daylight was when movements were most likely to be spotted from the air. The enemy made use of the fact that the American Army did not normally fight at night.

11. The enemy knew that when the helicopters were flying low, an insertion was going to take place somewhere in the area. Our adversaries were determined, dedicated, motivated, well disciplined, well trained, and very resourceful.

These were the risks we took during our offensive operations.

1. Making an insert on a Landing Zone (LZ) occupied by enemy forces. There were a couple of operations where the team set down on an LZ that was part of an enemy base camp. Natural ground vegetation and excellent camouflage techniques used by the NVA made detection of people very difficult in many of the areas.

2. Doing an insert on an LZ when watchers were on it or near it. Guard posts were manned in and around many clearings that could be used for an insert. Temporary guards were posted in areas during times of high NVA activity.

3. Setting down on an LZ that was mined or booby trapped. Many sites that could be used, or were used in the past, were mined or booby trapped.

4. Having trackers pick up your trail soon after an insert. If a tracker picked up your trail right after an insert it was bad. If they found your trail a day or two later, you were usually extracted before they could find you.

5. Making unexpected contact with an enemy force. Making a planned contact was usually manageable. An unexpected contact usually resulted in an ambush or firefight. Immediate action drills were practiced to escape this situation. The drills were designed to allow a team to break contact with an enemy force and get away.

6. Making contact with or being seen by a civilian. There was no way of telling friend from foe by dress or actions. Being seen by anyone was a danger for the team. The only way to eliminate the danger was to not be seen or eliminate everyone who saw you.

7. Engaging an enemy force and not being able to break contact. Teams had minimal resources. The amount of ammunition and grenades a team carried was limited. So was food and water. A team's best form of defense was to run and hide. However, you could only run for so long before becoming exhausted. There were "go pills" or amphetamines in our survival kits. They allowed you to go several days without sleep. But your body and mind paid a price if you used them.

Several teams were lost because they were located by an enemy force, could not break contact, and were overwhelmed.

8. Engagement with a large enemy force and not having air assets available. Air assets were the best support. Air assets could pluck you from a bad situation and reinsert you at a new location. There were times when no support was available and all a team got were the words to break contact and continue the mission. No assets available were words we did not like to hear.

9. Becoming a casualty of Friendly Fire. Even though a "no fire box" was maintained around the area a team was operating in, that didn't mean that an accident wouldn't or couldn't happen. Most of the area along the borders was a free fire zone. That meant that a pilot flying above could attack anything that moved and looked like an enemy force. One of the things I hated to find in an area was a US Air Force cluster mine dispenser that appeared to be recently dropped. When you found one, you were never sure that mines had not been dropped in the area you were walking in. Finding a live mine would ruin your day!

10. The vermin that lurked in the jungle. There were mosquitoes that carried malaria, leeches, large ants, large spiders, poisonous snakes, large cats and feral hogs that hunted in the day and night. The threat from this area ranged from a nuisance to death. All bush soldiers in Vietnam faced the same threat. However soldiers in regular army units had medics with large first aid kits with them and were usually no more than an hour from a field hospital. In our situation, it took more time than that just to arrange an emergency extraction.

The vermin were a real threat. After one operation I became a med-evacuation patient to the field hospital in Cam Rahn Bay. I spent a week there with a high fever, chills, and severe muscle cramps. The diagnosis was FUO or Fever of Unknown Origin. The doctors said that the most likely case was from an insect bite. That period was probably the most fearful and uncomfortable week I spent in Vietnam.

I have been asked, "How could you jump from a perfectly good airplane?" And, "How could you just hop off a helicopter into enemy held territory?" I guess the answer is that people take risks every day. Every time a pilot starts a plane rolling down a runway, he or she is taking a risk. Every time a surgeon opens up a patient, he or she is taking a risk. Hell, every time you drive down a road, you are taking a risk. There are many risks that we take every day. They become a part of our life and we accept them. We take them so often that the risks become normal and we don't think about them anymore.

Risks come in many forms. To face them you identify what can go wrong. You train and plan to keep the identified things from going wrong. And when things do go wrong, you make it right the best way you can. Our ability to reduce the risks was due to our determination, dedication, motivation, discipline, better training, better assets and support, and modern equipment.

2

THE MISSIONS
AND THE RULES OF ENGAGEMENT

The mission was to find and monitor the movement of enemy soldiers and the equipment they carried or to locate where he was assembling and hiding his supplies. Our mission was not to fight enemy soldiers. The mission was not to kill. The mission was to sneak in, find useful information, and then get out with that information so it could be acted upon. Our force, a six man team, was small. It was much too small to engage enemy forces on their own territory. There was one caveat to avoiding contact and a fight. And that was if the chance to capture a high ranking officer or adviser presented itself, we could act on that chance if the risk of loss of the team was not high.

There were four basic mission guide lines for all of the operations. The first was to carry out the mission unobserved. Physical contact with the enemy or the civilian population was to be avoided. The second was to eliminate those who did see you. There was a simple reason for this. The teams were operating in the enemy's back yard and you could not know who was friend or foe. For the safety of the team and the security of the mission, it was easier and safer to eliminate anyone who could report seeing you or threaten you with a weapon. The third was to leave no American behind. For morale and mission security, men who supported the recon teams died trying to extract live and dead comrades. And the fourth was that clothing, gear, and equipment was to be sterile;

nothing was to be carried that had US markings or identified you as an American soldier. Recon personnel were not to carry ID cards, dog tags, Geneva Convention Cards or anything else that would identify them as American soldiers. If any of the rules were violated, this one rule was violated the most. Many of the men laced a dog tag to one of their boots.

I can imagine some of you gasping as you read the mission guidelines. That's not sporting! American troops didn't do such things. American soldiers would not shoot someone just because they were in the wrong place at the wrong time. If where we were was a normal battlefield I would agree with you. If we could tell the civilians from paramilitary helping the NVA, I would agree with you. If we were carrying military ID and Geneva Convention cards, and in a US Army uniform I would agree with you. If I could be sure that I would not have had my hands and head cut off if the NVA captured me, I would agree with you. If my government was going to announce how and were we were killed (if that happened) I would agree with you. But none of that was the case.

The vast majority of people in and around the trail networks were working for or under the control of the NVA. Secondly, there was no minor torture and then a POW stockade for us if we were caught. What awaited us was down right bone crushing treatment and then a trip to the unknown. To put it mildly, we were not appreciated by those we searched for and spied on. A Studies and Observation Group (SOG) soldier was never paraded in front of North Vietnamese cameras! They didn't survive long enough for that the happen.

Under these conditions, eliminating someone because they saw us was not an issue. Shooting someone from behind or from cover with a silenced weapon was not an issue. What was an issue was completing the mission and coming home without anyone else knowing we had crossed a border.

Having stated all of that, the only time we (the team I was on) encountered a civilian face to face, the civilian was allowed to go on her way. She was not harmed. The standing guideline of eliminating all who see you was not enforced. We just got out of the area quickly and changed our direction of travel several times. We took the risk and everything worked out. The teams were generally so good in avoiding unwanted contact that these types of encounters didn't happen very often. We were more likely to bump into soldiers than civilians.

There were additional reasons for our guidelines. The knowledge of an agreement between the US and that of Cambodia for operations along the border was something our government wanted to keep quiet. This meant that the military actions in Cambodia also had to be kept from the US public and from the North Vietnamese.

Although the objective of every operation was to gather information, the specific goal of each operation differed based on the intelligence and the level of activity in a given area. All operations were planned and directed with a specific purpose in mind. The first objective was basic information gathering. It was accomplished by an insertion into and the reconnaissance of an area to see what use the enemy soldiers were making of the area. It usually included the dedicated watching of a road, river, or trail in a specified area. It always included information on the vegetation in regards to tree and ground cover, streams and water sources, food resources like fruit and crops, civilian traffic, and the width and types of trails. Intelligence is information that has been analyzed. It is like fragments that are pieced together to form a picture. We gathered a lot of information.

The second was a bomb damage assessment (BDA). The team was inserted into the targeted area one or two days before the bombing. The team would move unobserved to a designated point that was a safe distance from where the B-52 strike was going to take place. As the last bombs were falling they received a signal to move out. When they reached the targeted site, they conducted a search of the strike area to document the effectiveness of the bombing. They identified what had been destroyed and made an estimate of the number of casualties. It was not uncommon during these operations to encounter dazed and shell shocked North Vietnamese Army soldiers. These live soldiers were dispatched as quickly and quietly as possible.

The general recon and bomb damage assessment (BDA) accounted for most of the operations. However, there were other dedicated missions. When intelligence indicated that a high ranking officer or foreign advisor was in an area, a team was sent in to find and remove that particular person or persons. The mission was to capture him if they could or kill him if they could not. Some missions involved looking for allied prisoners or a known defector. Other missions called for the recovery or destruction of sensitive equipment or the planting of and retrieval of sensors.

The search for American POW's was always a priority. When intelligence indicated the US soldiers were being held in an area, teams were inserted to find them. Almost all of these operations ended with no prisoners being located much less liberated. The reason for the lack of success was due to the POWs being moved to another location before the intelligence could be acted upon. Despite the constant failures, the attempts were always made.

I know of two operations where the focus of the operations was to locate a US service member who had defected and was reported to be working for or with the NVA. The defector was rumored to have been a private in the Marines. The who and why is unknown to me. But there were stories about a handful of US personnel who went AWOL and or defected while in country. I can not remember any information or stories about any of these defectors being caught. Several teams reported hearing commands given in English when contact was made with NVA units. Just how accurate or reliable those stories were is open for questions.

3

HOW THE OPERATIONS WERE CONDUCTED

The terrain in Cambodia differed from area to area and hence in operation to operation. The mountains in the northeast and east of Cambodia flowed down and merged with the Central Highlands of what was then, Cambodia and South Vietnam. The topography ranged from a rugged mixture of mountains, ridgelines and valleys to gently rolling, almost flat ground.

The tree coverage varied from a thick tropical rainforest of double canopy jungle, to a single canopy, and in some places it became a widely broken canopy. The ground cover or vegetation varied as well. You could be dropped on a small clearing and then find yourself in vegetation so dense that you could not see twenty yards ahead. On the next operation you would think you were in an open grass covered savannah with scattered sections of trees where you could see for hundreds of yards.

A map of this terrain was on one wall of the briefing room in the tactical operations center (TOC). The map covered all of South Vietnam and the bordering countries of Cambodia, Laos, and North Vietnam. This map was divided into ten by ten kilometer squares. Each of these squares was a target area that was monitored by aerial photography, signal intelligence, sensors, and by putting boots on the ground. All of these target areas had a designation or identifier that consisted of a letter and a two digit number (example H-51). In a file cabinet was a file for each of these pieces of terrain. If the file for a specific area wasn't in our TOC, it was in the tactical operations centers of one of the other Studies and Observations Group (SOG) compounds. In the file folders were photographs and copies of the reports from each team that had ever entered these 10 by 10 kilometer squares. All of the information ever generated on each piece of terrain was available for a team being prepared to enter that specific piece of terrain.

Each operation began with a decision made miles away. On a side street in Saigon was a compound with the designation of Op-35. The men and women who worked there were the funnel through which the after action reports from the different SOG compounds flowed and new reconnaissance targets for the compounds were selected. The selection of a target area was based on what was indicated in the analyzed information that came in from all over Vietnam.

There was also an Op-31, 32, 33 and an Op-34. They may have been in the same location as Op-35. What they controlled is unknown to me. Talk around our compound had them controlling such things as psychological operations, maritime operations, and infiltrations into south China and North Vietnam. I only know that Op-35 was the controller for the recon teams and Mike Force based at CCS (Command and Control South), CCC (Command and Control Central), and CCN (Command and Control North). There are so many bits and pieces of information and disinformation about SOG floating around that it is sometimes difficult to put it all together. Because of this, I can only provide information about what I saw, heard or took part in where I was stationed.

At Command and Control South, deploying recon teams normally consisted of two Americans and four mercenary scouts. Six to seven indigenous scouts were assigned to a team, but usually only four at a time accompanied the two Americans on an operation. The most experienced American on a team was the team leader and held the designation of One-zero. The second American usually carried the radio equipment and was designated as the One-one. If there was a third American on an Operation he was the One-two.

The mercenary scouts were generally indigenous to the area and included Rhade Montagnards, Mnongs, Nungs, and a few Chieu Hoi. The Rhade, Mnongs, and Nungs were tribes of people who lived in the central highlands. Chieu Hoi's were NVA or VC that for some reason had a change of heart and were now working for US forces in South Vietnam.

The teams had names. In our case the names were tools. Recon team Hammer, Saw, Nail, Ax, and Level are examples. The teams at CCC were named after states in the US. I think the teams at CCN had names of animals or snakes. This was done so a person reading a report at Op-35 would know where that recon team was based just by reading the team name.

When the program originally started at CCS there were eight teams. By the time I arrived, the program had been expanded and there were twelve to fourteen teams. About half of that number would be on the ground during any given week. Two or three teams would be getting ready to go in. Two or three would be resting because they just finished an operation. And one or two teams would not be available due to illness, injury, R&R or an administrative action; an example of which would be a promotion board.

The normal activity cycle for a recon team lasted about two and a half weeks. It started with the assignment of a mission. The team was given three or four days for preparation. This prep time started with a mission briefing where the team was told were it was going and the scheduled insert date. The mission briefing included detailed information on the possible locations of enemy forces, available assets, and what the mission was to accomplish. This was followed with the studying of maps, photos, and the reading of intelligence reports, and previous mission reports on the targeted area.

Within a day or two of the mission briefing, the team leader made an over flight of the target area with a FAC (Forward Air Controller) to select infiltration points and extraction points. Photographs were taken of the selected insert and extraction sites. The photos were used in the mission briefing and provided to the air assets so they would know what the selected areas looked like. The rest of the prep time was taken up with any special training that needed to be accomplished, immediate action drills, the cleaning and a function check of weapons, the issuing of needed supplies, the packing of rucksacks, and a brief back to the commander and S-3.

The brief back, a detailed mission briefing given to the commander by the recon team, consisted of a verbal briefing on the goals of the mission, who was taking part, selected insert and extraction points, insertion plans, planned directions of movements, equipment taken, topography, expected vegetation and type of jungle canopy, water sources, and emergency plans.

The briefing went into great detail and included information like who would be sitting where in the aircraft during flight, who would exit on the different sides of the aircraft, and who would do what if problems arose. The brief back was a measure taken to ensure that everyone knew his part and responsibilities in the mission. It was a verbal walk through of everything that had been planned and actions to take if things went wrong. After the brief back, the team moved to a launch site. Launch sites were normally located at or adjacent to A-camps and other compounds near the Cambodian border. Then, at the scheduled time, the team was inserted and conducted their assigned mission.

Operations were normally planned to last between five to ten days. Some operations were shortened by contact that couldn't be broken. Not being able to break contact resulted in the team being pulled out before the mission was completed. Many times a team that was pulled out was immediately re-inserted into the area to continue the mission. On occasions a team would go past the scheduled extraction date due to weather or assets being diverted for use in another area. You could just about plan on being on the ground for a week at a time give or take a day or two.

Upon extraction, the team returned to camp and was debriefed. After conclusion of the debriefing, the team was given two to three days off to rest and then the cycle started all over again. Except for stand downs, teams were being inserted and or extracted on a daily basis. The rest and prep times were compressed at times when action was heavy and teams were in short supply. But for the most part, the general schedule was pretty much adhered to.

This normal cycle was only broken three times during the year I was there. There was a two week stand down (cessation of operations) in the fall of 1968 when a couple of teams were shot up and or lost during their inserts. The stand down was assessment time to figure out what went wrong. The second stand down occurred in the spring of 1969 when a Cambodian military unit was shot up. I don't know if a recon team mistook the Cambodian unit for NVA and called in an air strike or if they bumped into one another and a firefight ensued. Either way, a number of Cambodian soldiers were killed and wounded. The Cambodian government got hot over it and it took about three weeks for diplomacy to work the thing out. The third stand down came in the wet months (May through October). It rained so hard and the visibility was so bad that operations were halted for almost two weeks.

At the start of an operation, pants were bloused into the tops boots and then taped. This was done to help keep out leeches and insects. It also limited the changing of dirty socks or underclothes. What you wore on the first day, is what was normally worn for the duration of the mission. Extra clothing was not considered a necessity. No one wanted to get caught changing clothing along the Ho Chi Minh Trail. No one wanted to be literally "caught with their pants down".

On the ground, teams walked in single file. The first person in the file, or point man, was usually an indigenous scout. The indigenous interpreter followed the point man. Behind him was the One-zero and the One-one. An indigenous scout followed the One-one and the trail gunner brought up the rear. Each team member had an assigned area to search while they were moving and a designated action to perform if unexpected contact was made. This order of movement differed slightly from team to team. Some tram leaders, the One-zero, like to follow the point man. But the basic configuration with the Americans in the middle was the one most often followed. It placed the two Americans together in the center of the team. And it provided for the most control.

When a regular army unit went on patrol a squad leader or platoon leader was normally in charge. The leader would designate someone to be a pace man. This person would keep track of the distance covered when the patrol was moving. Another soldier would be designated as a compass man. This individual would keep track of the direction of movement. The leader was free to maintain over all control and watch for items of interest. On our teams, the One-zero did all of this. He kept track of the distance covered. He maintained the compass heading. He maintained control of the point man and kept watch for items of interest or danger. A soldier in SOG had to be proficient with a map and compass and skilled in orienteering to make it on a recon team. A team could not afford not to know where they were at all times.

The teams were active and conducted movement or searches from dawn to dusk. Activity along the trail networks went on day and night. The NVA and VC were active during the night as well as the day. Repairs to damage from bombs and artillery fire were often made during the night time. This was the period when they were least vulnerable to observation and interdiction. During daylight hours we were less likely to bump into enemy soldiers. Teams could hear them before seeing them as they talked and joked in their rest areas or while walking the trails. The odor of cooking food was often a sign of being near a base or rest camp. There were times when operations and searches took place during the night time hours. But for the most part, teams searched during daylight hours.

The teams did all they could to remain undetected. Steps taken to remain undetected went so far as to worry about the odors released when voiding or defecating. It was standard practice to bury trash and urinate in streams to reduce the chance of detection. Some team members went to the extremes and took medications to reduce the urge to defecate in an effort to reduce detection. It was not uncommon to have to take a laxative upon return to the compound following an operation. Speaking was limited to whispers in the RON (remain over night) sites. On the move, communications was through hand signals. Except to check for their use, trails and ridgelines were avoided. Because of the terrain and the need to avoid contact, if a team moved four or six kilometers in a day it was thought to be moving quickly.

At the end of a day, the One-zero would select a place to spend the night. The team generally moved past that selected spot and then circled around to come back to it. This was done to check the team's back trail to see if trackers were following. Once the team was settled into that selected spot, which was normally the thickest area of vegetation or the most difficult area to get to, the One-zero would encode a message that gave a rundown of the day's activities and the location of the RON position. The message was intended to let the command know were the team was in case a problem developed during the dark hours and to provide any information that could not wait until the team was extracted.

The team's location was important for another reason. The areas the teams operated in were usually free fire zones. To keep the team from being stuck by friendly fire, a 5 to 6 kilometer square "no strike box" was maintained around the team. The box was moved as the team moved. Without the box, teams could have been fired on by friendly air and ground assets. Staying inside the "no strike box" was an additional reason for the slow methodical movement that did not cover a lot of ground from daylight to dark.

Real sleep did not exist on an operation. For someone not raised there, the jungles of Southeast Asia are full of strange but natural noises. Monkeys and birds played in the trees during the daytime. All manner of animals and snakes, large and small, walked or slithered through and hunted in the vegetation at night. Tigers, panthers, feral hogs, wild ox, bears, deer, a variety of snakes and the Asian elephant made their home in the jungle. The slightest noise was a cause for alert. Was that noise a wild animal hunting pray or was it a breeze blowing through a stand of bamboo? Was it a poisonous snake? Or was it a man hunting you and your teammates? On a mission, rest and cat naps were about all your system let you achieve in the way of sleep.

Someone was always wide awake while in the RON. A team did not want to be surprised in the morning. And there was always a need to have someone awake to kick the leg of those who started snoring, moaning, or groaning. Some teams let 50 percent sleep while the other 50 percent maintain a watch. Other teams kept one man awake while the rest slept. We had two people keep watch while the other four slept. Six hours was about all the time there was for sleep. You moved into the RON as daylight was fading and everyone was up and awake before daylight arrived. Once you stopped there were meals to eat, notes to write, and a message to prepare and send. Before dawn there again was a meal to eat and a message to prepare and send. The team had to be ready to face anything once daylight arrived. Real sleep came when you got back to the compound. It was not uncommon for soldiers to sleep twelve to fourteen hours after returning from a long operation.

At first light, the One-zero would compose and encode a message indicating the status of the team, anything that had happened during the night, and the direction of travel for that day. After the One-zero sent the message, the daily activities would begin. After eating, you put on your rucksack and it stayed on the rest of the day. You didn't remove it until you settled into the RON site that night. And there were times, in areas of high enemy movement, where you slept with the rucksack on. During these times, you rested by sitting down, leaning back against your rucksack, and napping the best you could.

Meals were normally eaten in the morning before departing the RON site and in the evening after moving into a RON site. All meals were eaten cold. Fires and heaters were not allowed. They created aromas that could alert someone of our presents. And they were an unnecessary weight. At times the meals were eaten dry, with much crunching, and followed with a half canteen of water to make it easier to digest. Hard candy was often carried as a between meal snack and to reduce the feeling of thirst. The foil wrapper from the meals and other such trash was buried at the RON site and the disposal spot was camouflaged before the team moved out.

Water was carried in as many canteens as an individual felt comfortable carrying. Once on the ground, water was obtained from whatever source was available. The source was usually a mountain stream. But if need be, water was collected from a pond or bomb crater. Iodine tables made the water safe, but did nothing for the flavor. Water was needed for drinking and to reconstitute the freeze dried meals we carried. We filled a lot of canteens during one of our walks in the woods.

In the movies, everyone is wearing camouflage paint on their faces and hands. Camouflage materials were available. But I can't recall anyone wearing the stuff. I am sure that some teams did. I didn't. The other team members I knew didn't. The idea behind all the operations was to go in and not be seen. If you took the care and patience to move the way you were taught, you remained unseen. Therefore, no need for camouflage sticks. If you were seen at a distance, you wanted to look as much like an NVA patrol as possible. They didn't wear camouflage in their areas. So again, there was no need to wear face paint.

In all operations, regardless of the dedicated mission, the teams performed the basic recon mission of gathering and recording information on people in the area, man made structures, food sources, water sources, trails, and types of vegetation they encountered. This saturation patrolling produced a significant amount of intelligence and placed significant pressure on enemy units. The pressure applied was sufficient to cause the North to put bounties on the killing or capturing of SOG recon personnel.

Along with the gathered information on the movement and buildup of NVA units and camps, assessment of damage done on the ground by air strikes and the elimination of a few high ranking officers, the operations had other successful affects. The first was the effect on enemy soldiers. Our operations let them know that they were not the only ones who could play the hide and seek, hit and run game. American soldiers and news reporters in South Vietnam referred to the VC and NVA as ghosts in the jungle. We were the ghosts for the NVA in Cambodia. Tens of thousands of enemy soldiers were tied up guarding areas and searching for our teams. Estimates of the number range from at least 70 thousand to over 100 thousand. These were enemy soldiers that would otherwise have been free to move into South Vietnam and engage our soldiers and ARVN forces.

Another affect was the psychological mistrust of their weapons and the destruction of enemy weapons during their use. Teams, on almost every mission, carried "doctored" (booby trapped) Soviet or Chinese ammunition. These munitions, code named Italian Green, would explode when fired. Imagine firing your rife during an assault and having it blow up in your face. Or drop a 61mm mortar round down a tube and have the tube explode taking out everyone around it. We planted this stuff in caches, dropped it along trails, or left it on the edges of enemy base camps. Anywhere we thought an enemy soldier was likely to find and later use it became a salting point.

For a period of time, I hated carrying the stuff. But one night our compound came under attack. Minutes into the attack, from off in the distance, there came the sound of an explosion. The mortar and rocket attack stopped. The next morning, a patrol found what was left of a mortar tube and several unfired mortar rounds. It never bothered me to carry the stuff after that. No matter how much other equipment I had to carry, I looked forward to planting or dropping the Italian Green.

American soldiers, upon arrival in country, were told not to fire a captured weapon until the weapon could be inspected and found safe. They were told that many weapons used by the Viet Cong and NVA were hand made or assemble from odd parts and this made them unsafe. This was a cover story to hide the real cause of enemy weapons failures; the doctored ammunitions dropped along trails or placed in enemy caches by special operations teams.

Any Grunt worth his salt would have had an issue with this excuse. The American M-16 was like a well machined high compression engine that requires high octane gas to operate. It requires a trained individual to repair or swap pieces. The Soviet or Chinese AK-47 was like a sloppy diesel engine that can use diesel fuel, an oil and gas mixture, or even the oil from a fast food fryer to run. The AK-47 was designed so a soldier on the battle field could take parts from broken or damaged weapons and piece them together to make a functioning weapon.

The other thing we dropped from time to time was a small portable radio. The radio worked. It would receive on one or two frequencies; one of which was a US run South Vietnamese propaganda station. The other thing it did when turned on was transmit a signal. Surveillance aircraft (black birds) tracked the signals from these radios. If a signal was tracked moving southward along one of the major trail networks, the location of the signal was targeted with an air strike.

The most dangerous periods of any operation were the insertion and the extraction of the teams. The noise of the aircraft attracted attention. The aircraft were large targets for every weapon in the area. You were never sure that you were not being observed by someone every time you hopped off a helicopter. If a team was able to move off the LZ and not make contact with anyone for thirty minutes or so, the team had a real good chance of not making any unexpected contact during the duration of the mission. When it came time for the extraction, the thought was always in the back of your mind that there could be an enemy force set up somewhere near by and they were waiting for the slick to come in before springing their ambush.

Skill, motivation, and daring all played a roll in these missions. Luck also played a part. On one operation, a team that had been inserted into an area to check on a suspected increase in activity awoke in their RON site to commands being given in Vietnamese. When the team leader asked his interpreter what was being said, he was told that the companies were being called to attention. They had stopped their search the previous night within a couple hundred yards of a large enemy base camp or assembly area.

If a team followed the basic procedures taught to all the teams, their chance of staying unobserved were pretty good. The basics rules consisted of the following:

1. Do not walk on trails or ridgelines.
Walking on trails or ridgelines was easier and allowed a team to cover ground more quickly. But it greatly increased your chance of being seen, found, and compromised. It also increased your chance of stepping on a mine or booby trap.

2. Never travel in a straight line from point to point. Traveling in a straight line allowed an enemy force to determine a likely route and set up an ambush. You were never positive that the enemy didn't know you were there.

3. Circle back and cross your trail to check for trackers at least once a day. This was the only way a team could check to see if the team had been compromised and was being trailed.

4. Move slowly, deliberately, and stop often to listen. Movement created noise. The slower the movement the less noise was made. Deliberate movement avoided stepping on sticks, crushing small plants, or overturning stones and debris that left a trail. Stopping and listening let you tune in to what was going on around you.

5. Pay attention to the natural animal noises and movements around you. The unnatural daytime movement of nocturnal animals could tell you if someone else was in the area. So could the chatter of monkeys and birds. The absence of all animal sounds during daylight hours was also a clue that other humans were somewhere in the area.

6. Don't make any fires to heat food or to get warm. Fire, smoke and hot food created odors that could be detected a long ways off.

7. Don't talk while on the move. Sounds are carried a long ways. Sounds seems to exceptionally noticeable in a world devoid of cars, trucks, radios, and people traffic.

8. Don't eat while on the move. Don't do anything while moving that distracts from you ability to look and listen to what is going on around you.

9. Don't smoke. The odor of cigarettes is carried a long way.

10. Stay focused. In the RON you can eat,

whisper, think about other things. While on the move, thinking about or doing anything that took your attention away from your ability to see and hear is foolish and deadly.

Failure to follow the basics usually caused an unexpected contact with a civilian or an enemy force. Daniel Boone and Major Robert Rogers, of Rogers' Rangers fame, would have felt at home on a SOG recon team. While the use of helicopters would be strange, the operations on the ground would have been familiar. Major Rogers issued the following standing orders to his Rangers:

1. Don't forget nothing.

2. Have your musket clean as a whistle, hatchet scoured, 60 rounds powder and ball, and be ready to march at a minute's warning.

3. When you are on the march, act the way you would if you was sneaking up on a deer. See the enemy first.

4. Tell the truth about what you see and what you do. There is an army depending on us for correct information. You can lie all you please when you tell other folks about the rangers. But don't never lie to a ranger or officer.

5. Don't ever take a chance you don't have to.

6. When we're on the march we march in single file, far enough apart so one shot can't go through two men.

7. If we strike swamps, or soft ground, we spread out abreast, so it's hard to track us.

8. When we march, we keep moving till dark, so as to give the enemy the least possible chance at us.

9. When we camp, half the party stays awake while the other half sleeps.

10. If we take prisoners, we keep 'em separated till we have had time to examine them, so they can't cook up a story between 'em.

11. Don't ever march home the same way. Take a different route so you won't be ambushed.

12. No matter whether we travel in big parties or little ones, each party had to keep a scout 20 yards ahead, 20 yards on each flank, and 20 yards to the rear, so the main body can't be surprised and wiped out.

13. Every night you'll be told where to meet if surrounded by a superior force.

14. Don't ever sit down to eat without posting sentries.

15. Don't sleep beyond dawn. Dawn is when French and Indians attack.

16. Don't cross a river by a regular ford.

17. If somebody's tailing you, make a circle, come back onto your own tracks, and ambush the folks that aim to ambush you.

18. Don't ever stand up when the enemy's coming against you. Kneel down, lie down, hid behind a tree.

19. Let the enemy come till he's almost close enough to touch. Then let him have it and jump out and finish him with your hatchet.

The skills and tactics we used were known and used by our early frontier men. Tracking, walking in a single file, checking your back trail, avoiding trails and ridgelines, living without fires and comfort, striking your enemy quickly from cover and then getting away to fight some other place was used by our soldiers in the French and Indian Wars. About the only difference between our operations and theirs were the meals, the clothing, the weapons, and the fact that Daniel probably spent the night under a wool blanket and we rolled up in a poncho or poncho liner. When you think about it, life for a scout hasn't really changed that much.

The missions of scouts in Daniel's days were very similar. They conducted patrols and monitored the movement of enemy forces. They searched for new routes of travel and mapped them for use by friendly forces. They set up ambushes and made raids for psychological and physical gains. They acted as messengers. Those old skills and tactics used by Daniel Boone and Major Rogers are as useful today as they were three hundred years ago.

Studies and Observation Group (SOG) teams and support came from a number of services. Navy and SEAL team members, Marine Recon, Army Rangers as well as Special

Forces and Air Force personnel made contributions. Insertion means, team personnel, and team size varied with each organization, where they were located, the area of operations, and the mission. However, US Army Special Forces personnel were the backbone of SOG operations.

On three occasions my team went to Command and Control Central (CCC) and Command and Control North (CCN) compounds to support operations from those locations. Those three operations were much different from what was done at our home base. The areas of operation there were more rugged in regards to hills and vegetation and the target areas were more heavily populated with enemy soldiers. The teams from those compounds experienced more contacts and firefights. The tactics and the make up of teams were different. The mission insertion aircraft were old CH34 Kingbee helicopters flown by Vietnamese pilots and the tactics they used scared the hell out of me.

What an operation was like and "were you afraid" are hard questions to answer. Fear runs the gamut from left side of the brain simple apprehension to right side of the brain screaming, crying and breaking down. Feelings and emotions are the result of chemical and electrical stimulation in the brain. Everyone is different. No two people think the same or feel the same emotions. Flying at tree top level may scare the hell out of some and not others. Getting into a firefight might bring fear and mental shutdown to a few but is exhilarating to others.

I don't think that fear intruded into our work very often. People commit crimes. They wouldn't commit crimes if they believed they were going to be caught. They know that people do get caught, but they don't think it will happen to them. Soldiers work with the same thought pattern. Yes teams did get caught. Soldiers and friends did get killed. But it will not happen to me. When fear surfaced, when it became a present conscience thing, it was a signal that it was time to leave a team. Apprehension made people cautious. Fear made people ineffective.

For me, each mission started with some anticipation of what general location was the target area going to be? What was the expected level of activity? And what was the purpose of the mission? It was kind of like what you would feel while waiting to go on rollercoaster ride that you have never ridden before. I would describe it as a mixture of anticipation and anxiety. Somewhere in your head is the knowledge that sometimes people get hurt doing this, but lets get on with it because this is fun and I won't get hurt today.

The next two or three days were filled with the individual tasks of getting ready. After the brief back and I started putting on my load bearing equipment and my rucksack, the butterflies started flying around in my stomach. This feeling was not fear but anticipation of the unknown. Once I boarded the helicopters for the ride out to the launch site, and or the ride to the insert point, almost all feelings melted away. My thoughts were full of too many other things. I was too busy searching the ground below me for activity, man made structures, trails, and streams. I thought about what I was going to do if contact was made on the LZ or what would I do if it was mined? Once on the ground, analyzing what I was seeing and hearing left little room for any other thoughts.

A handful of the soldiers I served with in Vietnam were in the Guards and Reserves. They had volunteered for active service as well as for duty in Vietnam. They did not have to be there. The only thing that explains why there were so many volunteers is that most of us were thrill seekers and adrenalin junkies! In another life we would have been pirates, mountain men, gunfighters, or explorers. We were not the kind to work eight to five behind a desk, wear a dress uniform or a suit and tie every day, or be a general's lackey in the Pentagon. We were soldiers who wanted to do what we had been trained to do. And the only place available was the war in Vietnam.

Questions abut the CIA often comes up when the talk turns to special ops. Was the CIA involved? The answer is yes. The father of the CIA was the Office of Strategic Services (OSS). The OSS was involved in military operations and efforts to gather intelligence during World War II. OP-35 was the control center for CCS. It was the control center for CCC and CCN as well. The physical location was in a compound on a side street in Saigon. A black in color, eight foot tall solid metal fence with a twelve foot tall chain link fence above it hid the compound from the street. The link between the military run operations and the CIA was there. This was where the information gathered by the teams was sent and from where operations were directed.

There is one final thought about fighting, learned from an old sergeant major, which guided me and many of my friends during our operations in Vietnam and throughout my military career. There is no honor in fighting. There is no shame in losing. There is no code for the great warrior. You don't get extra points for being a gentleman. In any fight, strike quickly and hit hard. Disable or kill your opponent before he can harm you.

4

THE SOLDIERS

Among those who never served there, the Vietnam War is difficult to understand. Service and the military ethos are even difficult for some of those who fought there. Why would soldiers volunteer to go to a combat zone and risk being crippled or killed? The question becomes even more difficult to understand when the soldiers were not physically protecting their family and homes. Thousands of soldiers volunteered to serve in Vietnam. Many of them volunteered to go more than once.

Special forces soldiers were in Special Forces units because they wanted to be there, because they were intelligent (it was easier to qualify for Officer Candidate School or any other school the Army had than Special Forces), and because they were very skilled in their specialties. They all had to have volunteered for Airborne training and completed it. They had to have volunteered for Special Forces and passed the rigorous screening and training. Commitment to Special Forces and the Army was important to the men who wore a green beret.

That commitment is reflected in two things I was told during my first year in Special Forces. The first was that you could lie and steal from a "leg" (a non airborne soldier). But never lie or steal from a fellow Special Forces soldier. The second was instructions from a sergeant major that if it was sometimes necessary to bend a rule or regulation to get the mission done, you do it. And that if you were caught breaking the rules; you would be all right as long as it was done for the sake of the mission and not for personal gain. That is the way it was. That was the attitude.

There was also another attitude. The desire to serve and do what one was trained to do. Places where you could get away from the daily routine and do some of the things you were trained to do were limited. Most of my friends volunteered to go to Viet Nam. Southeast Asia was a place where you got to do some of the things you were trained to do. I volunteered to go and was turned down. My military skills were not needed. I ended up going to school to obtain another Military Occupation Specialty (job skill) so that I could go and experience what my friends and team mates were all talking about.

There may have been a need buried in me somewhere to have a ribbon or two to display on my uniform. Or I may have been expressing my desire to go where the action was, a desire to seek adventure, or a search for the unknown. After all, guys who had been to Vietnam were volunteering to go back. There had to be something good there or the guys in the know would be avoiding the duty. Whatever the motivation, I and other Special Forces soldiers were volunteering to go where many of our citizens and soldiers were fighting to avoid.

Once assigned to SOG, all American recon team members went through RECONDO School. The training was called the Recon Team Leaders Course. The instructors were experienced members of Project Delta. Most of the training provided there wasn't new material for Special Forces soldiers. But it was a good refresher course for topics such as map reading, land navigation, weapons, and it provided practice for how the inserts and extractions would be accomplished. Most of the indigenous scouts had been with the Civilian Irregular Defense Group (CIDG) programs and were very experienced in combat operations. These CIDG units were formed and trained by Special Forces personnel to fight the Viet Cong in their local hamlets. Many of them had years of combat experience.

The following is a piece of writing I saw on the walls of a club. I don't remember exactly where I saw it but I am sure it was in Da Nang or Kontum. It describes the early days pretty well.

THE SPECIAL FORCES SOLDIER AS SEEN BY:

MILITARY ASSISTANCE COMMAND-VIETNAM: A drunken, brawling, jeep stealing, woman corrupting liar with a star sapphire ring, Rolex watch, and a demo knife.

HIMSELF: A tall handsome, highly trained professional killer, female idol, sapphire ring wearing, demo knife carrying gentleman, who is always on time due to the reliability of his Rolex watch.

HIS WIFE: A stinking member of the family who comes through Fort Bragg once a month with a sack full of dirty clothes and a hard on.

HIS COMMANDER: A fine specimen of a drunken, brawling, jeep stealing, woman corrupting liar with a star sapphire ring, Rolex watch, and a demo knife.

DEPARTMENT OF THE ARMY: An overpaid, over ranked tax burden, that is indispensable because he had volunteered to go anywhere, do anything, as long as he can booze it up, brawl, steel jeeps, corrupt women, wear a star sapphire ring, a Rolex watch, and carry a demo knife.

Author unknown.

I have been asked what my age was when I served in Vietnam. I was twenty-two when I arrived and twenty-three when I left. The average American team member was probably in his late twenties to early thirties. Almost all were sergeants in the pay grades of E-6 or E-7. Everyone was in great shape. If you weren't in shape, you were weeded out during the in-processing and acclamation phase in Cam Rahn Bay. The average indigenous scout on the teams was probably mid to late thirties. I say probably because they lived hard lives and may have appeared older than their years. Age and physical condition was a discriminator.

War by nature is a young man's game. Daniel Boon was in his late thirties when he went exploring for opportunities in what was to become Kentucky. He had one asset we did not have and that was the use of a horse. He didn't have to walk all the time or carry everything on his back.

These then were the men who went to Vietnam, established and maintained camps and compounds in isolated areas, and volunteered for special ops. They were the cream of the crop! They were the best the Army had to offer. All of these men had very high test scores, outstanding physical and mental endurance, and the ability to think and reason. They were a brotherhood of soldiers with a mindset similar to the French Foreign Legion.

These were intelligent soldiers who were trained to fight and kill. Yet their main mission was to train and instruct others, and to build as well as destroy. Here were men who were ready to take off the uniform and set aside their military ID and Geneva Convention cards; men who were ready to bend rules and make new ones if the situation called for it. Men who were ready to go anywhere the mission required, and men who were ready to perform overtly or covertly to accomplish whatever their government asked of them.

5

WEAPONS AND EQUIPMENT

What would Daniel have carried on his trips west into what is now Kentucky? He probably wore a wide brim floppy hat, loose fitting wool or muslin shirt, and wool or cotton pants with an adjustable tie string opening in the rear. His armament could have been a .75 caliber British Brown Bess flintlock musket. However, it more than likely was a .50 to .54 caliber rifle made by a gunsmith in Pennsylvania. In addition to the rifle, he would have carried a large knife, and maybe a small hatchet.

In addition to the weapons, he would have carried lead balls in a hunting pouch that hung from a wide leather belt. Next to the hunting pouch would have been a flint and steel pouch that carried spare flints and a vent pick for his musket or rifle. A set of powder horns or flasks would have hung from leather or hemp cords that crossed his chest and back. In a large shoulder or possibles bag he would have carried some bacon, jerked meat, corn meal, and hardtack biscuits. For a source of water he would have carried a metal flask or a wooden canteen. A rolled up wool blanket, tossed over one shoulder, would have contained an extra shirt or jacket. All of this would have had a weight of 20 to 25 pounds.

When you arrived at Ban Me Thuot from Nha Trang, you arrived with your personal items and an M2, .30 caliber carbine. During in-processing, you turned in the M2 and were issued a new weapon and a variety of equipment. In my case, the issue was a compass, a new Seiko watch, a "SOG" knife, canvas rucksack, load bearing harness, three canteens, a survival kit, an emergency radio, a Browning High Power (9mm, semi auto pistol), an American M16 rifle, and a Soviet or Chinese made AK-47 assault rifle. Within a very short period of time, I had added an M3 "grease gun" with an attached suppressor and had a case of claymore mines, a case of grenades, a case of .45 auto ammunition, time fuse, blasting caps, and fuse igniters under my bed.

The M16 was issued for camp defense. It did not take long to learn the difference between an M16 firing and the noise an AK-47 made. An American soldier did not want to be inside the compound firing an AK when the camp was under attack. Life would get very difficult if you were mistaken for a sapper who had gotten inside the compound. For the same reason, the M16 wasn't taken on any operations. For these two reasons the M16 didn't get used very much. It went with me to a fighting position when the camp was under attack. I used it when running or practicing immediate action drills. For most of my tour, the M16 gathered dust while hanging on my wall.

The AK-47 and the suppressed or silenced M3 were carried on operations. The type of mission, and my role in it, dictated which weapon I was going to carry. The Browning was my constant companion. It went where I went. On operations it was in a holster. At other times it was stuck in the waistband of my pants. I never left the compound without it. At night, in the compound, it lay on the footlocker next to the head of my bed.

Each American team member carried a rucksack, a survival kit, survival radio, knife, water and food for ten days, weapon and ammunition, and any other equipment that was necessary to complete the mission. The indigenous team member carried their weapons, ammunition, food and water. Normally no extra clothing was taken. Comfort items were limited to a poncho and poncho liner. In the dry seasons, the poncho was left behind. Nothing was carried that didn't pertain to safety, security, survival, and mission accomplishment. The bare minimums!

The survival radios were carried by both American team members. They were the same radios issued to air force pilots.

Air force aircraft or pilots were all we could talk to if we used them. We had them in case our back pack radios failed or they were damaged or lost during a firefight. The only time I used one was during training in RECONDO School. Having them on an operation increased your sense of security. The survival kits contained such things as extra water purification tablets, amphetamine tablets, a wire saw, a signal mirror, fish hook and line, and some high energy candy.

Toilet articles were usually limited to a toothbrush that was carried in a shirt pocket. The only other item of clothing that some teams carried was a black nylon jacket. Sown into the back of the jacket was a pouch. This pouch contained a pair of black nylon pants and an orange panel. If your world really turned to crap, you could pull on the jacket and pants, crawl out into a section of tall grass, pull the panel over you and hope you were seen from the air and not from the ground.

Meals were normally LRP's or long range patrol rations. While the rest of the soldiers in Vietnam were eating C-rations out of small green cans, we were furnished freeze-dried meals that one ate from a plastic pouch after pouring in some water and letting them sit for ten to fifteen minutes. Each meal was lightweight and compact. There were eight different entries. Chili con carnie, spaghetti with meat sauce, and chicken and rice are the flavors I remember most. Along with the main entry were a powdered beverage, cereal bars, cookies, and an accessory pack. All we packed were the main entry and the plastic spoons. Two meals a day provided us with about 2200 calories. There were meals specifically packaged for the indigenous personnel on the team. These indigenous meals were basically fish and rice or squid and rice and they tasted pretty good.

In addition to these basic items, other items were obtained from supply. During the dry months, 35mm black and white film and Pentax 35mm cameras or Penn EE-S2 half frame cameras were issued to record things of interest seen on our walks across the borders. During the wet months, Nikonos waterproof cameras were used. Small compact field glasses, radio equipment, batteries, rations, explosives, non electric blasting caps, and sterile uniforms were also supplied as needed.

Claymore mines are anti personnel mines that are directional. They can be fired using electrical or non electrical firing systems. They were designed to be used as a perimeter defense weapon or in an ambush situation. When fired they discharge some 700 small steel balls into a fan shaped area. The claymore mines we used were set up and carried with non-electric fuses. Usually three or four of these mines were carried with fuses cut for burn times of 30 seconds, one minute, two minutes, or three or four minutes.

The burn times varied with the team leaders and what they thought they may need. The purpose of carrying the mines made up this way was to have the ability to just pull one from the outside of a rucksack with a minimum of preparation. It was set facing the direction you had just traveled, the fuse ignited, and the mine left with the hope that the trackers or enemy soldiers that were following you walked up to it as it was exploding. Even if it went off too soon, it slowed the trackers and or trailing soldiers down and discouraged their rapid advance.

Some teams carried claymore mines and their firing wire to set up outside their RON sites at night. We didn't do it. We didn't think it was worth the time and effort to put them out and pick them up again in the morning. Claymore mines were also carried to set up ambushes or a snatch. A technique was taught where two claymore mines were set out facing away from each other. When the person you wanted to snatch was in the middle or centered between the two mines, both mines were fire at the same time. The back blast was cancelled out where the two forces met. And every one in front of the two mines was eliminated. We practiced setting up the mines in this fashion but never used the technique. We never had a situation where we could!

Three types of silenced weapons were available to the teams. The first was a High Standard, .22 caliber, semi auto pistol with a built in suppressor. The second was a .32 caliber Berretta with a detachable suppressor. And the third was the trusty M3, .45 caliber grease gun. Noise suppressed weapons like these were of little value as offensive weapons. Sights, a long effective range, and a high volume of fire were non existent. For the same reasons they were almost as useless as defensive weapons. Their value was in the ability to eliminate someone, at close range, without attracting a lot of attention. The suppressed weapons were limited in number and usually only became available for issue as one was turned in at the departure of another team member.

Most teams had someone trained to carry and use the M-79 grenade launcher. It was a good weapon to have around in a firefight. Up close, the buckshot rounds were good for breaking contact. At longer ranges, it kept the enemy from getting too close. Almost everyone carried fragmentation grenades. I carried two along with four white phosphorous grenades. Because of their weight, the willie peter grenades were hard to throw a long distance. But they got the enemy's attention when you tossed one and they exploded.

If you wanted to try them, there were other weapons available from supply. The variety available ranged from a couple of World War II M1 Garand rifles and a BAR to a few Russian or Chinese rifles and submachine guns. If you wanted something really silent, there was a bow and some arrows or a couple of crossbows and bolts. But I can't recall anyone taking them on an operation. There were some fighting knives and tomahawks as well. But I think all they did was gather dust.

In between operations, everyone wore the standard green jungle fatigue uniform with all the unit patches, rank, and name tags sewn on. For operations there were three different uniforms available. The first was the regular green jungle fatigues. The second was the tiger strip fatigues. The third was a gray green uniform that may have been French military equipment or a copy of the NVA uniform. In all cases these uniforms were worn without name tabs, rank, and unit patches. For headgear, most teams wore the camouflaged tiger striped boney hat. A few individual had captured NVA caps or helmets. They wore them in place of the issued headgear.

The rucksack that was issued was an indigenous canvas rucksack with three outside pockets. It wasn't as large as the American rucksack or as comfortable. But it resembled the bag used by the NVA and it did the job. Looking like or being mistaken for an NVA squad, when seen from a distance, was what you wanted. If the team was observed and the enemy was unsure of whom you were, it increased your chances of getting away.

Most of the load bearing harnesses were made of cotton fiber. A few of the newer nylon harnesses with quick releases were issued too. While I was in country, a new load bearing harness became popular. The harness had additional straps sown to it. Two thick wide ones were at the shoulders and two smaller ones were on the rear of the belt. If you were going to be extracted by rope, you pulled out the two straps at the belt and routed them between your legs and attached them to the front of the belt. This made a seat. The straps at the shoulders were pulled out and hooked with a snap link to the rope that was lowered from the helicopter. With this new system, you could be extracted and have full use of your hands and weapon while being pulled up and out of a hot spot.

There was one major issue with issued equipment. It was the 7.62 X 57 ammunitions for our AK-47's. Because of the doctored AK ammo that was dropped, special care was taken with all AK-47 ammo. Once a can of the "safe" ammunition was opened, it was loaded into magazines and the rest was expended. Loose rounds were not left lying around for fear of good and bad ammo getting mixed. Normally the doctored munitions were issued just prior to packing and departing the compound. If you found an AK magazine with live rounds in it, you removed the rounds and destroyed them. No one wanted a mistake made with the doctored ammo.

Some team members carried handcuffs in case they captured an enemy soldier. Others carried sections of rope for the same purpose. I carried about 50 feet of parachute cord. It was light, didn't take up much room, and was very strong. Out of the whole year I was there, I can only recall one incident where a team came back with a prisoner.

There were some items carried by a few teams that were not issued items. A few teams had rubber stamps made and they would stamp the forehead or hands of those they made contact with in the jungle. A couple of teams carried the aces or kings from decks of playing cards. They would leave them next to or on people they made contact with in the jungle. While the mission was to get in and get out without anyone knowing, if a team had to leave evidence of our being there, such as a dead body, we wanted the NVA to know it was from us. It was our version of psychological warfare. No doubt these actions caused some intimidation and were the bases for some of the extra hostility towards us.

6

SUPPORT

Some would think that sneaking into enemy held territory and looking for enemy soldiers would be a scary thing. It wasn't. It wasn't for a number of reasons. Most of the reasons were connected to the support we received. Teams penetrated up to 30 kilometers deep into the countries bordering South Vietnam. This was the area where the Ho Chi Minh Trail was located. It was where rest and training camps, supply caches, and staging areas were located. This 20 to 30 kilometer wide strip was the pipeline for troops and equipment that was re-supplying the NVA and Viet Cong in South Vietnam.

Support for our operations came in many modes. The first and the best came from the US Air Force's 20th Special Operations Squadron. These crews provided the helicopter support for our inserts and extractions. The helicopters crews that supported our operations wore sterile clothing. The helicopters used in our operations had a tail number but no other military, or Air Force markings. The only identification was a green hornet painted on the tail boom. The aircraft flew into and out of our compound to support our operations. And although there were parking revetments for them, they seldom stayed there over night. The air crews preferred the luxuries of their own compound to ours.

The danger they faced was greater than what we faced. The threat was the same but the probability of a deadly encounter increased for them. A team made an insertion and extraction about every two to three weeks. These guys faced them daily with every team that went in and came out. The odds, that they would encounter a hot LZ or extraction, were much greater than ours. Plus the aircraft they manned were a larger target. It was known that the enemy would prefer downing an aircraft as well as getting a recon team. It is believed that they often followed teams in hopes of ambushing the team and helicopters during an extraction. What can I say? They were great! They were fantastic! In truth, the words are not there to express how dangerous and stressful their jobs were or how well they performed. Maybe it is enough to say that team members owed their lives and freedom to the men who manned these aircraft that dropped us off and picked us up.

There has not been enough praise for the pilots and door gunners of the slicks that dropped us off and picked us up and for the gunships that turned more than one hot extraction into a cool one. Not enough has been written about the guts and dedication displayed by these aircrews. Many a recon team came back because these professionals said to hell with the enemy fire, and came in and snatched teams out. Several of these helicopters and crew members were lost in attempts to extract surrounded teams. Men doing other jobs in other areas of Vietnam, received awards for doing once what these air crews did daily; which was going into some place under fire to pick up or pull troops out of harms way. The fact that we knew that if our world turned to shit, these crews would come and attempt to get us out, cast the enemy threat into a totally different light.

A second form of support was Command and Control (C and C). A small fixed wing aircraft was in the air during the morning and evening hours. In the plane was a pilot and staff officers from our compound. We knew that if we needed help in a hurry during daylight hours, this asset was there to call on and the staff in it would send the assistance that was needed. There were times when a call was made for an extraction and the answer from C and C was to continue the mission. That didn't happen very often. But when it did, you did the best you could with what you had, and you hoped their decision was the correct one. In most cases though, when the bullets were flying and you called for an extraction, the support was massed to get you out.

If anyone could be considered the cavalry, the forward air controllers (FAC's) could. A FAC pilot was in the air and along the border during most of the daylight hours. A call for help was answered almost immediately. Get into trouble and a FAC could have fast movers (jets) or slow movers (prop and rotary aircraft) overhead within a short period of time.

Planned inserts and extractions were put on hold when a team was in trouble so that available assets could be diverted. While the called for aircraft were en route, the FAC would verify the team's position by having the team pop a smoke grenade and or a visual fly over. He would then mark the enemy positions with rockets for the "big boys" when they arrived.

It was not uncommon for one Major to fly his plane in such a manner as to be able to fire a handgun or rifle out the window in an effort to draw some of the enemy fire away from the team that was in trouble. When he told a One-Zero to "pop smoke and stand on it", the team knew to close ranks and get low to the ground because the ordinance was going to come in close. The Major was good. I think most of the FAC's were ex jet jockeys and did all they could to get close and mix it up with the enemy.

These pilots also deserve more recognition than they have received. People talk and write about the air crews delivering ordinance on a target, killer teams getting out and doing their bad deeds, or aircraft taking fire while dropping off troops on an LZ. Few think or write about the lone pilot, flying a slow fixed wing airplane, who coordinated all that action.

If your world was really turning black, there was a mobile strike force or Mike Force on standby to come to your aid. These units were trained in unconventional warfare operations. They did very well in the role for which they were trained; which was raids, ambushes, reconnaissance and rapid reaction. They did not do as well when conventional unit commanders tried to use them in the basic infantry role for extended periods of time.

One of the uses of the Mike Force was to assist in the extraction of teams in trouble and as a force of opportunity to engage identified enemy forces. These indigenous soldiers, led by Special Forces soldiers many of whom had also served on recon teams, would chopper or drop in and engage enemy forces that were attacking a team. Many times, for them, it was like David taking on Goliath. You just had to hang on long enough for them to arrive.

A not too much talked about form of support were the C-130 and C-123 black birds that were in the air from dusk to dawn. The special warfare planes got their name from the black camouflage paint they displayed and their roll in the war. The main mission of the planes was electronic surveillance along the border. Among other things, the planes carried detection and intercept equipment and dropped sensors. When they were in the air, which was daily and nightly, it was a source to relay messages or request fire support. It was comforting to know that a friendly voice could be there in the dark of night when things could turn bad. There was also a radio relay station with the call sign of Hammerhead that could also be reached 24 hours a day.

During the hours of darkness, the fixed and airborne relay stations were the only real support available. If anything happened during the night, everyone would rush to your aid in the morning. The cavalry did not ride at night. After the sun went down, you were on our own except for radio contact and maybe some artillery fire.

The last form of outside support that could be called on was artillery fire. Fire bases were scattered along the border areas. And from where they were located, their guns could reach well into some of the areas the teams operated in. The 155 howitzer were almost useless to us. However, the 8 inch howitzer could reach out about ten and a half miles and the 175 mm artillery gun could touch someone out to around twenty miles. Most of the areas the teams went into, artillery support was not available. In those areas where it was available, fire support firing at max extreme ranges wasn't the most accurate. However, when the chips were down and support was needed, an artillery barrage, even at max ranges, was a whole lot better than nothing.

The artillery pieces were also a threat. Every night sections of terrain were picked out and artillery and mortar rounds were fired into these selected areas. The areas were called free fire zones. And the fire was called H and I or harassment and interdiction fire. These were rounds that were just lobbed out into an area in the hopes that enemy troops would be there. These free fire zones existed throughout Vietnam and the border areas. I don't know how effective H and I fire was. But the pockmarked ground from where these rounds landed was visible during any flight over the countryside.

In a way, the enemy paramilitary forces, gave us some support. That is if you call giving information to the enemy support. The trackers and the soldiers chasing us often used rifle shots to communicate. A team would be moving and they would hear a rifle shot from an area they had moved thru. Then an answering shot or two or three shots in quick succession would come from another area. This would go on, two shots from your flank and then a shot from some other another location. I don't think most teams knew exactly what those shots were communicating. But they generally meant that you had trackers on you tail and someone else was trying to move in to set up an ambush or establish blocking force.

I can't leave the subject of support without mentioning the support that we gave each other through our training and the desire to get the mission done. Not wanting to fail in the eyes of your peers is strong motivation. That feeling is what keeps many going in combat. When you get right down to it, men don't fight for the flag or mom's apple pie. They fight for each other. No soldier wants to let his friends down or appear to be a coward in their eyes.

In the years following Vietnam, I never heard one soldier say they volunteered for a tour in Vietnam to fight for the United States. I can't recall anyone saying they went to fight for democracy. What I did hear was "that's were the good duty was", "that's where all my buddies were", or "those poor Vietnamese bastards needed some help".

We were all volunteers. To get there you had to have volunteered for airborne training, Special Forces, and special ops. All one had to do to get off a team was to say he wanted off. Although one would be asked why, your wanting off was the end of the story and the command found another job for you.

7

LIVING CONDITIONS

Our living conditions must be considered a part of the story. If you look at the amount time spent in the compound between operations and the amount of time actually on the ground conducting an operation, you would soon realize that we spent about forty percent of our tour sleeping in our bunks and sixty percent in the jungle. I think that when most people think of serving in Vietnam, they have visions of Kha Sanh and the marines living in mud holes and being continually pounded by mortar and artillery rounds. They recall the movie and TV news scenes of unshaven and out of uniform soldiers sloshing through rice paddies while on patrol. Or they envision dirty men sleeping in tents and slugging it out with companies of NVA infantry. There were Special Forces soldiers who lived in camps without running water. There were soldiers who slept in metal shipping containers buried in the ground and went on patrols looking for a fight with the enemy. We didn't live that way. And we didn't fight the war that way.

On a mission we lived like Daniel and his consorts must have lived in enemy territory. Cold camps! No noise! And minimum comfort! In our compound it was a different story. We slept on real beds with clean sheets. We showered in real shower stalls with hot and cold running water. The soldiers I served with showered and shaved daily when they were in the compound. Clean pressed uniforms and shined boots were the order of the day. Many of the soldiers, sailors, and marines fought the war this way. Pilots got up, showered, dressed, ate a hot meal, climbed into their aircraft, flew their missions, and came home to cold beer and clean sheets. Sailors did the same thing. It really was a different war for us.

Meals were prepared in a real stateside like mess hall using a lot of fresh meats and vegetables. Movies were shown two or three nights a week in our air conditioned club. Maids made our beds and washed our clothes. Short timer calendars were present. Peace symbols were not. Living in our little camp was almost comfortable.

Bear in mind that when I joined the army, a barracks was a World War II era two story wooden structure with a large open bay upstairs and downstairs. Each bay was filled with bunk beds. The latrines were open rooms with eight to ten sinks, six toilets, a trough urinal along one wall, and a single shower stall with six shower heads. Privacy did not exist. Comfort was not an issue.

Everything you owned had to fit inside a standard footlocker and a metal wall locker. The only other place you could keep things was in the trunk of your car. When I arrived at Fort Bragg, North Carolina, home of Special Forces, all of our buildings on Smoke Bomb Hill were World War II structures. There was no such thing as air conditioning. Heat in the winter time was available through old boilers that had to be fed coal every few hours. Considering what I was accustomed to and that we were not living in tents, our compound was quite comfortable.

The Command and Control South compound, that I called home, was a rectangle that measured about 150 yards wide and 900 yards long with the long axis running east to west. Outlining this rectangle was a six foot high earthen wall. This berm was about four feet wide at the top and eight to ten feet wide at its base. Dug into this earth work were the fox holes and reinforced bunkers from which the camp defenders stood guard and fought off the ground attacks that seemed to come every two to three months. In reality they occurred less often than that.

On three corners of the compound were wooden observation towers that reached some thirty feet above the almost flat but gently rolling terrain upon which our camp was constructed. Outside of the earthwork were belts of barbwire obstacles, trip flares, and mines. Beyond the warning wire was the dusty brown earth and patches of low growing vegetation that belonged to the Vietnamese and the Viet Cong after dark.

Far off in the distance, yet visible on the horizon, were the mountains that surround our small section of the central highlands. Their mass was always darker than the sky and they were only obscured by the heavy rains and an occasional plumb of smoke that usually meant someone was getting attacked.

Between our camp and those far off mountains, only one item broke up the sameness of this view. It was a hill. Located to the northeast about a mile away, this five to six hundred meter high and a kilometer long mound of brown dirt and thick vegetation dominated the gently rolling terrain around it. At night the land between our camp and the hill was a free fire zone. Anything that moved in the area after dark could be and often was fired upon. H and I or harassment and interdiction fire, consisting of mortar and artillery rounds, was an almost nightly occurrence. The small craters created by the H and I fire dotted the ground in this free fire zone.

The gate, and only entrance into our world, was on the east side of the compound. The road from our front gate went east, past the control tower and airfield that was located about a mile away, and on towards the city of Ban Me Thuot (Buôn Mê Thuột), the 23th Infantry Division Headquarters, and the MAC-V compound. East of the airport, the road branched towards the northwest, passed the hill, and on to some small Vietnamese towns and a Montagnard village. A hundred yards or so from our gate, the road curved south towards the artillery compound that shared our southern perimeter. It continued on around the end of the runway and on towards the south and past an army combat engineer compound that was located some 15 to 20 miles away.

In the mornings, a long line of locals walked up to the gate to have their ID cards checked. Old men and women in black pajamas stood quietly among young girls in their brightly colored dress. Slowly they would move forward and few words would be spoken. Once inside the compound they would call out greetings to people they knew. The young girls would laugh and cover their faces when the American soldiers called out to them. These local people cleaned our barracks, made our beds, cleaned the latrines, worked in the mess hall, repaired buildings, dug and maintained fighting positions, and a sundry other labor intensive jobs around the camp.

The command estimated that at least ten percent of this workforce was VC. If any of them were VC, you couldn't tell it by their actions and activities. They worked hard and were friendly. If they had any faults, it was that some tended to take things that weren't nailed down. One thing that seemed to regularly disappear was boot socks. When a significant number of the indigenous workers left early or failed to show for work. Camp defenses went on an increased alert status.

The eastern end of the compound was where the American and Vietnamese Special Forces troops were housed. It was also the area where the supply building, club, mess hall, motor pool, and generators, were located. The supply building was one of the largest buildings in the compound. The mess hall was a close second. The motor pool was small. I think it consisted of a 2 ½ ton truck, an ambulance, two jeeps, a 5/4 ton truck, and two ¾ ton trucks. Two very large diesel generators supplied the electricity for the compound. The only time one of them wasn't running was when the camp was attacked.

The club was about 20 by 50 feet with a long bar along the south wall. A dozen or so card tables and a pool table filled up the rest of the room. Movies were projected on a screen on the west wall and an office and supply room occupied the east end of the building. The club was a place to socialize; a place to discuss operations and tactics. Walking into the club was like walking into a piece of America. I can not recall ever seeing a Vietnamese civilian, soldier or other indigenous person inside its walls.

The western end of the camp was where the indigenous soldiers, Mnong, Nung, and Rhade Montagnard mercenaries, maintained their living quarters. Their buildings were similar to those we lived in. We all lived in wood framed, plank sided, 24 by 60 foot long structures. Outside the buildings looked the same. Same wood, same design and an almost equal number of sandbags stacked around the structures to provide some protection from incoming rounds and explosions. But there were significant differences. Inside, our barracks were sectioned off into individual rooms. A hallway ran the length of ours with doors that provided entrance to the ten by ten foot rooms. Their buildings were open bays. We slept on a mattress on a metal cot and they slept in hammocks. On hot nights we all sweated. On cool nights, we had blankets.

Behind our billets were western style bathrooms. We had flushing toilets and hot water showers. We also had three French toilets. These were nothing more than a sewer pipe with tile around it. You made use of them by squatting over the open pipe and defecating. The mercenaries had a hose for a shower. And for a bathroom they had outhouses. Every other day or so, the air would be filled with the smell of burning shit as the waste in these outhouses was mixed with diesel fuel and burned. The only irritation we experienced with our bathrooms was the need to clean muddy footprints off the toilet seats. The indigenous personnel like our bathroom but they wanted to stand on the seats and squat. The same way they did with the French toilets.

In between these living areas were the mortar pits, headquarters building and TOC (tactical operations center), aid station, and the helicopter landing pad and parking revetments for the aircraft that supported our operations. The landing pad was just about in the middle of the compound. In the dry seasons, every incoming and departing bird kicked up dust storms of the powdery red earth. This helped distribute the stuff all around the camp. Everything was covered and stained by it.

Most Special Forces A-camps and compounds in Viet Nam were stuck out in the boonies by themselves. These camps were manned by Special Forces teams and a trained force of indigenous people. They were generally scattered near the border areas. We were somewhat lucky in the fact that an artillery company shared the space between us and the end of the Ban Me Thuot airport runway.

I say somewhat lucky because while they guarded our southern flank, and were always ready to trade rations and beer for war trophies, their eight-inch howitzers and 175mm guns were constantly firing across our camp. And their ammo storage facility, just off the southwest corner of our camp, drew constant fire from enemy rockets and mortar tubes. I often felt that the incoming rounds that we received were actually meant for the artillery compound and their ammo storage facility.

Life within the compound was almost pleasant. It was definitely relaxed. Major attacks, aimed at the compound were few and far between. The occasional sniper or barrage of rockets and mortar rounds did little damage. The threat of harm was there but not high on the radar screen. The personnel assigned to support the camp caught most of the physical threat. Their fighting positions were on the three exposed sides of the compound. Recon personnel were assigned fighting positions that joined with the artillery company. This was a necessity because no one knew who or how many recon people would be in the camp when it was attacked.

The food in the mess hall was some of the best I've ever eaten. We ate a lot of fresh steak and other meats. I think this eating well was at the expense of other soldiers in country. Our supply and mess people were always trading stuff that had been picked up on operations for rations, beer, cokes, and other things we enjoyed. It was also possible that some of the items traded originated right there in our compound. I know that some of the trade items, like flags and bows, were made by the families of the indigenous scouts in our compound.

Recreation consisted of pinochle or poker games, billiards, volleyball, basketball, jogging, reading, writing, or getting a box of ammo from supply and shooting a weapon from the berm into the open spaces west of the compound. A basketball and volleyball court was located between our barracks buildings and the mess hall. But they didn't see a lot of use by the recon personnel. Preparation days didn't leave much time for playing. And a lot of after operations off time was spent sleeping and resting.

Most off duty recreation and socializing took place in the club. The air-conditioned building opened officially at 1500 hours. However, the doors were unlocked at 1000 hours and the pool and card tables could be used. You just couldn't get a cold beer until three o'clock in the afternoon. With the air conditioning, beer, movies, card tables and pool table, the place attracted a lot of attention. It was a great little spot that never seemed to run out of cold coke, cold beer, and snacks.

Every now and then, someone would check out a jeep or 5/4 ton and a group of guys would go into town for a meal and Vietnamese beer. The trips into town often included a stop at one of the steam baths where an attractive looking young lady took your money and an old crone, with betel nut stained teeth and gums, gave you a massage. A real get away trip was accepting an invitation to one of the local villages for a meal and some rice wine. If you were invited, you almost had to go. To decline without a "real" reason not to go was a disgrace to the indigenous person who invited you.

Duty wise, life in the compound was almost like being in the US. You were expected to shave daily, get a hair cut once a week, and wear a clean and serviceable uniform and shined boots. In other words, you were expected and required to look and act like a soldier. On Monday through Saturday, the first formation was at 0700 hours. The evening formation was at 1700 hours. Sunday there was no formation but it seemed like any other day of the week.

At formation time, you fell into one of three platoons. One of the platoon ranks were filled with the radio operators, cooks, clerks, medics, and mechanics. These were the people who kept the camp running and provided support for the operations. A second platoon was for the camp security troops. These soldiers pulled guard, supervised the local workers, manned the camp's main weapons, repaired wire obstacles, laid new mines, and led patrols into the area immediately around the compound. The third platoon ranks were filled by the recon teams. There was an additional platoon in the formation. And it consisted of the LLDB, the Vietnamese Special Forces, which were assigned to our compound.

Professional soldiers don't a whole lot to be happy. Meaningful work, honest leadership, decent food, friendly faces, provisions to stay clean, a place to get warm when its cold and dry when its wet is all most soldiers really need. The compound provided all of this and more. What needs it didn't supply could be bought at the small Post Exchange at the MAC-V compound, the Base Exchange at theUS Air Force compound located at the Ban Me Thuot city air field, or bought on the local economy.

Welcome sign at airport

Sign above barracks door

Recon Team Nail, 1st quarter of 1969

RT Nail running immediate action drills

Cleaning weapons after an operation

Typical jungle LZ with trails in forground

Section of Ambush Alley

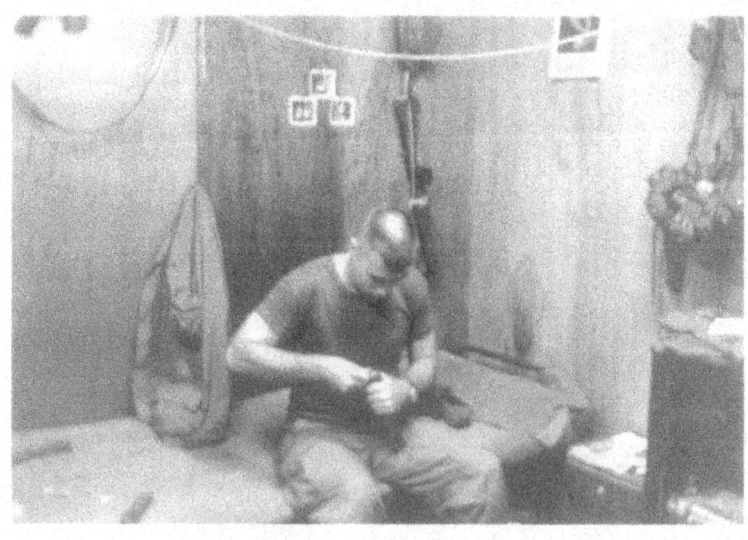

Loading magazines for the silenced M-3

20th Special Operations Squadron gunship

FAC airfraft at the Bon Me Thuot ariport

One form of recreation

Our counterparts, the LLDB

Coming out on a rope.

Names on new sidewalk

8

INSERTIONS

Getting into a target area was accomplished by several means. At times, teams walked into an area. They would be mixed in with a platoon or company of soldiers that was making a sweep on or near the border. At the appropriate time and place the team would walk away from the larger force and get lost in the jungle. The platoon or company would continue on and then return to camp.

Anyone watching would not know a team had slipped into an area. In the northern areas teams sometimes used parachutes to get on the ground. In the delta area, teams often used Navy swift boats. But the most often preferred means of insertion was by helicopter. It was the quickest and most often the safest. Aircraft differed from area to area and from types of operations. In some areas, old Sikorsky CH34 helicopters, flown by Vietnamese or American pilots, were used. In our area, we had HU-1F/P helicopters (Hueys) flown by US Air Force crews.

The landing zones (LZ's) were small clearings in the jungle that were large enough for a helicopter to hover over. Some were made by man; a few were from bombing and or fires, and the rest were made by mother nature. The clearings were selected from the air based on indicators of little or no human activity in the area. The amount of activity could be gauged by the number and size of trails near the clearing and damage done to the vegetation on or near them. Clearings with a high speed trail or a large number of low speed trails near them were avoided. Almost all of the clearings had knee to waist high vegetation growing on them.

The term Landing Zone is used loosely. The helicopter never sat down or landed. They hovered anywhere from two to five feet in the air and the team jumped when told to do so. The last one or two team members jumping from the aircraft were exiting the doors as the helicopter was pitching forward and starting to gain altitude.

Our Hueys would take off from the launch site at dawn or near sundown. Early morning and late afternoons were the primary insert times. A gunship would fly in the lead position. Behind the gunship would be a slick, a cargo or personnel carrying helicopter, carrying the recon team. In trail behind the second bird would be another slick. And bringing up the rear would be a second gun ship. The four aircraft would fly in a staggered formation at a high altitude, out of range of RPG's (rocket propelled grenades) and small arms fire. The helicopters would cruse along until the flight was within twenty to thirty minutes of the insert point.

From a designated point, the flight would descend to treetop level and form up into a trail formation. Each trailing aircraft would fly about 30 seconds behind the aircraft it was following. Like a giant whirling, churning metal snake, the flight would weave, twist, and turn on the way to the designated insert point.

In the slick, behind the lead aircraft, the team leader sat on the floor (deck) at the door between a crew member (door gunner) and the back of the pilot's seat. With his feet hanging out over the skid, he held his weapon with one hand and held onto a metal frame member inside the aircraft with the other. From this position he could observe the ground below the aircraft and the area around part of the LZ as they were landing. He could also see the tops of trees flying by at eighty miles an hour during their approach.

The view, at times, was unsettling, especially when trees tops were flashing by that were higher than you were. On the other side of the Huey, the other American, the one-one, sat in the cargo bay in a similar position. The four indigenous members of the team sat between the two Americans.

About one minute out from the insert point, the crewmember would give the team leader a signal that the LZ was coming up. The leading gunship would cross the insert point and continue its flight. The slick with the team would drop to within two or three feet of the ground and the team would bail out. Three team members would exit on the port side and three others would bail out the starboard. The second slick and trailing gunship would pass over the top of the Huey dropping off the team. As the trailing gun ship passed overhead, the insert slick would drop his nose, gain altitude, and take its position as the last ship in the string of Hueys. The noise of the two aircraft passing overhead covered the noisy whop-whop sound of the insert. Unless there was someone at the insert point, it sounded and looked like four helicopters continuing to fly in trail.

The aircraft would fly on and maintain their twisting and turning flight for some 15 to 20 minutes. However, their flight path kept them within ten minutes or so from the drop off point incase the team got into trouble. If everything was alright on the ground the team would communicate that everything was okay by keying the mike on the radio two times. This keying the mike and not talking was called breaking squelch. If there was a problem the team would start taking on the radio. Voice contact meant problems and breaking squelch indicated everything was alright. Once cleared by the FAC after a successful insert, the helicopters headed back to refuel and what ever else was on their operations schedule.

The North Vietnamese regulars in the area were not dumb. They knew that choppers flying at tree top levels meant that someone was coming to pay them a visit. They just didn't know where. And it was not uncommon for them to have spotters stationed at clearings they thought might be used for an insertion. Nor was it uncommon to have spotters located along trails that led from clearings that could be used for infiltration or extraction. Their mining and booby trapping of clearings was more than just a nuisance!

To decrease the chance of enemy troops being on or near the LZ in areas of high activity, a deception was borrowed from WWII. When the airborne troops dropped into Normandy, dummies were also dropped at various locations to confuse the German defenses. That ploy was used in a number of our inserts. The choppers would fly to an LZ and use the normal insert routine. However, instead of a team deploying, four to six dummies would be tossed from the slick. The rubber and fiberglass dummies had small explosives charges (large firecrackers) imbedded in them that would start going off minutes after the helicopters left the area. I don't know if the decoys worked. We liked to think that they did.

The worst possible thing that could happen on an inset was to jump out onto an LZ that was occupied by an enemy force. That happened to two teams while I was in country. On one of the occasions, the LZ that the team landed on was in the middle of an enemy base camp. We lost the team, the slick that was inserting them, and almost lost a second helicopter. This situation was what most teams dreaded the most!

9

EXTRACTIONS

Just as with the insertions, there was more than one way of getting out. Some teams walked out. Some teams were extracted by watercraft. But mostly, teams were extracted by helicopters. Prior to insertion, the One-Zero would pick a primary and a secondary extraction point. If all went according to plan, one of those two points was where the team was picked up at the conclusion of the operation.

The extraction went in stages. The first stage occurred when the team moved to one of the extraction locations. When they arrived at the selected clearing, they would watch it for an hour or so to make sure the area was safe. The team would send a message that they were in place and ready; and then they would establish a perimeter and wait. This was a time when it the hardest to keep your mind on what was going on around you. Your thoughts tended to be on where was the aircraft and not on the terrain around you. It was a time when you could be feeling safe and the enemy was getting ready to take you out.

The second stage was getting the FAC on station. When the FAC got near, he would make contact with the team. If the FAC needed directions to pinpoint the team, the clock system was used to guide the FAC to the team's location. The nose of the plane was 12 o'clock. The One-zero could direct the fact or make corrections to his line of flight by tell him to fly a new heading based on the hours on a clock face. Telling him to fly 9 would cause the FAC to make a 90 degree turn to the left. Once the FAC had the team's position pinpointed, he would fly off and call for the extraction aircraft. The FAC flew off to keep from attraction attention. Orbiting a piece of terrain was likely to attract unwanted visitors. When the aircraft were en route the team would receive a radio call alerting them. The FAC would tell the incoming aircraft where the team was and which direction to fly to approach the pick up point.

The final stage was when the helicopters got near the team's location. The team would be asked if they had any company. A gunship would make a pass or two to confirm that the clearing was safe. Then a slick would come in, hover, and pick up the team. Most of the time, it really was as simple as waiting for the choppers to arrive, running out to board them, and then flying home. Even on those simple extractions where no physical contact was made with an enemy force, it just felt good when that bird lifted into the air and you knew you were going home.

Then there were the times when you would arrive at your extraction spot and all would be quiet. The gunship would make a pass and no shots would be fired. The slick would come in and start to hover and all hell would break loose. The extraction point would become hot and you would run and jump aboard the slick while gun ships made passes overhead to distract and suppress the enemy fire. I can't say those times were fun, but they sure caused big smiles and a lot of back slapping when you landed safely back at our compound.

Another type of hot extract occurred when you couldn't run to an open area large enough for a slick to get into. In this situation, the team was extracted at the end of a rope. A rope with a loop in the bottom of it, called a McGuire rig, was dropped to pick up soldiers in the situations where the helicopter could not set down. This initial rig became a large padded loop that would accommodate up to three team members at a time. In either case, you were carried away from your situation while hanging a hundred feet or so below the helicopter. No roller coaster on this earth will equal the adrenalin rush of being pulled up through trees and bamboo in a McGuire rig while people are shooting at you.

Getting into an area was easier than getting out. The enemy didn't know you were coming. If they somehow knew you were coming they didn't know where you would land. Once on the ground the situation changed. On the ground you had the chance of an encounter with a civilian, a paramilitary, or an NVA soldier or soldiers. There were trackers that followed you once they found your trail. There were watchers or guards; some of which watched trails and open areas from spider holes. With all of this to contend with, it is little wonder that many extractions were hot ones.

10

THE MIND AND BODY ADAPTS

    I didn't know it at the time but my body and mind began changing my first night in Vietnam. After landing at Ton Sa Nut airport in Saigon and going through customs, I boarded a C-123 with sixty to seventy other soldiers and took the short flight to Cam Rahn Bay. My first night there, I spent four hours in a bunker, waiting for an enemy attack. I was still dressed in my Class-B Khaki uniform. From then on, I was always conscience of where I was and what was going on around me.

    The body and mind can adapt to almost anything. That ability to adapt may be why we have been able to survive as a species under so many different living conditions. It is why we manage to do the things we do under a variety of circumstances and why the odd becomes normal. When thrown into a dangerous situation, our senses become more acute. Or maybe it is just that we pay more attention to them. I know I became conscious of new smells, new sounds, and any movement around me attracted my attention.

    The rucksack and load bearing equipment always seemed so heavy when I first put it on. The weight that I carried was normally in the range of sixty to seventy five pounds when I was a One-one. I carried about fifty pounds when I became a One-zero. The main difference in weight was a radio and extra batteries. An hour or so after putting on my equipment, it was like the ruck was no longer there. Or maybe I should say that its weight on my back seemed natural. The load was forgotten. I could and did wear it 24 hours a day without discomfort. It became a lesson in how the body and mind adapts.

The human sleep cycle is another area where we adapt. One can learn to sleep under almost any conditions. When I was the One-one and carried the radio, I would sleep at night with the radio handset next to my ear. If the radio broke squelch, I was instantly awake and could remember any call signs or voice message that had been transmitted. When I was in the camp, those 8 inch howitzers and 175mm guns next to our compound could complete a fire mission and I would sleep through it. But if there was the pop of a mortar round leaving its tube, I was immediately awake and my brain was calculating if it was outgoing or incoming. Sleep and noise acceptance are another amazing lesson in what the body and mind can adapt too.

When in the camp I ate breakfast, lunch, and a supper meal. If I skipped lunch, my system knew it and I became hungry. In the field I ate twice a day; once at dawn and once at dusk; and my system didn't seem to miss the lunch meal. There were no hunger sensations. It was if my system knew it was only going to get the two meals and it didn't object.

Soldiers adapt. If they don't get used to harsh conditions, they at least tolerate them. The better they understand the mission and respect their chain of command the greater the willingness to adapt and endure. It is sometime funny to see soldiers working in the rain as if it wasn't there because a mission calls for it and in other circumstances running to avid getting wet or not going somewhere at all because it is raining. Soldiers will endure work in high humidly and 110 degree temperatures and then complain because the air conditioning is set at 80 degrees. It has been said that it is a soldiers right to bitch and complain. It is and he does. A civilian or news reporter shouldn't confuse that complaining with a desire to not successfully complete a mission or a dislike of military service.

11

A DAY OF REALIZATION

Most people have a moment in their life when they realize something significant. It may be knowledge of their mortality. It may be a mistake they made or that they have done something really good without planning to do it. I had such a moment in Vietnam. It is funny or maybe I should say strange the different things that make an idea or concept sink in. Even though I had gone through two briefings where I was told that the operations were "all volunteer", that the missions were "secret", and that we couldn't talk about them to anyone outside our little group, the possible impact of this on my life did not register.

Being told that I could not talk about what was done, briefings on procedures such as sterile uniforms and no ID cards, and asked if I was sure that classified operations were what I wanted to do, just did not sink in until I was through with training and assigned to a team.

The realization of my new situation was like being smacked with a stick. About midmorning, on a day following my return from Recondo School and prior to my first operation, the light came on. The recon team to which I had been assigned was in the field on an operation somewhere across the border. I had walked down to an area near the front gate and was sitting on top of a bunker adjacent to the gate guard post.

Off in the distance, I could see a figure walking west along the road towards our compound. The sky was cloudless and a deep blue. The sun was heating up the ground and the dry air. The rising heat waves caused the walking figure to appear to shimmer and shake as if I was watching through a high powered scope or field glasses.

After a little while I could tell that the figure was an American soldier. Little clouds of dust rose and fell around his boots as he marched along the side of the roadway. In a few more minutes I could see the emblems on his shirt collar and it became obvious that he was an officer. When he finally got to the gate I could see that he was a Lieutenant Colonel and that he was an engineer. Sweat darkened the chest area of his shirt, his rolled up sleeves and his armpits. Dust covered his polished boots.

The sweat and dust stained officer's jaunty strides got him to the gate and he started to pass through when the American guard at the gate stopped him. I heard the officer state that he was waiting for a ride, his ride was going to be late, and he wanted to wait in our club and maybe get a drink if one was available. The guard told the officer that our compound was a restricted area and that he could not enter. The officer said something to the effect that he was a colonel in the United States Army, this was an Army compound, and that he could enter. The guard told the officer that he was sorry but the compound was off limits to everyone not assigned to it. The officer demanded to talk with the officer on duty. The sergeant picked up the phone, called the TOC, and then handed the phone to the officer.

The officer again explained that he was waiting for a ride, that he understood we had an air-conditioned club, and that he would like to wait for his ride there. I have no idea what he was told. But he made some comment about Vietnamese being allowed in the camp but not US soldiers and then slammed the phone down on the gate house table. The officer turned and started walking back towards the airfield while yelling back over his shoulder some not so very nice comments about Special Forces and how it fitted or didn't fit into the regular army.

I watched him walk back towards the airfield. The incident triggered thoughts I had never had before. I really was in a "special" compound. I was now a member of a very small, very special fraternity. Lots of soldiers were being assigned to duty in Vietnam. Many were wearing green berets. Only a handful was assigned to SOG. On previous walks to the supply building, I had noticed a sign that was propped against the side of a building. On the sign was the word Omega. The sign had hung somewhere not too long ago. I had never given it or my ending up here much thought. On this morning I did.

    A wave of doubt ran through my head. Could I successfully do what was being asked of me? Could I navigate as well as I thought I could? Could I carry my share of the load? I had two and a half years of training behind me. I had taught pre mission personnel during my assignment in B Company, 7th Special Forces Group. I had taken part in the dog and pony shows given at the Gabriel Demonstration Area on Fort Bragg. I was well trained! I had been training other soldiers on their way to Vietnam. I didn't wash out of Recon School. Why shouldn't I be able to do it! How really dangerous was it?

    In real simple terms, it sounded easy. Get on a chopper, fly to some spot, get off and walk around for a few days without been seen, and then get back on a chopper and fly back to camp. This had to be better duty than sitting in an A-camp somewhere. It had to be better than leading a Mike Force or running patrols with a CIDG company.

    Back in the states, veterans of Nam had talked of A-Team Camps, operations, and even Project Delta. No one had talked of Omega, Sigma, or the Phoenix Program. Six months ago, most of my buddies were receiving orders for Viet Nam. I volunteered to go and was turned down. Engineers and medics were not in great demand. Ops sergeants were. So I signed up for the Operations and Intel course. Three weeks after obtaining the 11F MOS designation, I received orders for the 5th Special Forces Group.

    How could I have so easily left my young wife and one year old twin daughters? If something happened to me, they would receive six months pay and twenty thousand dollars from an insurance policy. I had seen to it that they were in a new home on an acre of land that my wife's father had given us. The house would be paid for if I was killed or went missing. But, six months pay and twenty thousand dollars would keep them for about two years. It wasn't much of a legacy. Why hadn't I given more thought to their needs before becoming a volunteer?

Now I was part of something I couldn't write home about. I was part of something I couldn't brag about. Work was something I would have to keep from my parents, my wife, and my kids. A year or more of my life would have to be forgotten about when I left here. And if I died here, my family would never know how or why. Missing in action or died as a result of enemy engagement would be all they would ever learn.

These thoughts led me to others. How many other men who volunteered for Vietnam were having the same thoughts? How many would ever question their ability or wonder if they had made the right decision in requesting to come to a war zone? Full of piss and vinegar at 22 years of age, you don't ponder on such things for long. I didn't. I set the thoughts aside. What ever happened now was in God's hands. I would go home, or I wouldn't. It was as simple as that.

Thinking back on that day now, I know that young men are always volunteering to go off to war. War is a young mans game. Old men teach and lead, but it is young men who do most of the fighting. Youth does not consider the possibilities and the odds; they just do what must be done. Older solders also do what must be done. But they think more on the odd of things going wrong and the consequences if they do.

Daniel Boone was in his mid to late thirties when he made his trips from the Carolinas into the wilderness of Kentucky. He wasn't at war. But he faced war like dangers. Somewhere in all my reading, I read that he was captured during one of his several trips and held for an extended period of time before finally being released. In the back of my mind during my tour in Nam, there was always the acknowledgement that if I was captured I wouldn't be going home. That knowledge was extra motivation to try and do everything right.

12

PLANS CHANGE WITH THE FIRST SHOT

It is an old military axiom that plans last only as long as the first shot. What are some things that did go wrong? Teams landing on insertion points with enemy troops there! Support aircraft developing engine troubles at the wrong time! Intel officers not believing the information gathered by teams! Bad weather preventing the extraction of teams! Team members becoming ill after an insertion! These are things that could and did go wrong. The unexpected and the not counted for often popped up in the wrong places at the most inopportune time. For me, the most memorable example of this has to be the following.

The insert was a noisy but peaceful affair. Our flight path led us to one medium sized clearing and we followed the standard insert procedures; except we didn't get off the aircraft. Instead the flight crew in the aircraft trailing us kicked out four decoys into the middle of the clearing and took off again. While the noise generated by the decoys drew attention to that location, we inserted on a second clearing about three kilometers from the decoy site. The decoys were used because the area was believed to be a very active hot spot. All of the intel pointed to higher than normal activity. We were going to try and find out what that high activity was all about.

For three days we walked a zigzag course and found nothing. The terrain was rolling ground with a sparse single canopy composed of tall hardwoods growing among scattered clumps of waist to chest high ground cover. As far as finding signs of the enemy or the war, we could have been walking on the moon. On the fourth day of walking and not finding anything of interest, we found ourselves sitting on the highest piece of ground around us and watching the terrain around us.

The focus of our attention was a wide and well used footpath that ran in and out of the patches of ground cover. Our position was in a thick patch of waist high ferns located about 200 yards from the trail. We didn't know where this trail started or where it went. But we knew we were several kilometers from anything else that was considered part of the Ho Chi Minh Trail. The footpath was not marked on our maps. It was definitely being used and used heavily. The One-zero decided to spend some time and see who and what was moving along the pathway.

After several hours of surveillance, we were beginning to think that the trail wasn't used by anyone. That idea changed when a squad of NVA soldiers walked into view. Our attention was immediately drawn to what was with the squad of soldiers. It was an elephant. An elephant with a rider dressed in white. Wearing white pants, white shirt, white jacket, and a white hat, the rider appeared greatly out of place. A look through a pair of field glasses revealed the rider to be Asian. Was he Chinese? Was he a Soviet advisor or Vietnamese? Was he just a rich dude or an advisor? Why did he have an escort? There was only one way to find out. Capture his butt! Quickly we formed a plan based on the weapons we had.

The plan was simple. We would get ahead of them. When they came into range, we would use our 40mm grenades rounds to knock the rider off the elephant, take out his escorts with rifle fire and grenade rounds, and then collect the rider of the elephant and or whatever he may have been carrying. After working out this basic plan of action, and making sure it was understood by the indigenous scouts, we moved out to circle around and set up on the trail ahead of our victims.

After almost an hour of moving quickly and searching, we found a spot to our liking. In a clump of trees, about 100 yards from the trail, we waited for the party to come into view. In about 20 minutes we heard them coming up the trail. In another five minutes the little group appeared. Five armed guys were walking ahead of the elephant and two guys were walking on each of the elephant's flanks. The nine soldiers walking on the ground were talking. The guy riding the elephant was silent as he rocked forward and back in rhythm with the elephant's steps. Closer they came. I noticed the elephant's head was swinging side to side as he walked. The One-zero yelled now!

    Our indigenous scout grenadier fired his M-79 and we watched a puff of gray black smoke and flame erupt on the elephant's side. The sound of the exploding round reached our ears almost as quickly as the flash reached our eyes. The 40mm grenade round had struck the elephant high on his left side, above his rear leg, and no more than four feet from where the rider was sitting. The elephant tossed his head back, trumpeted, turned to his right and broke into a trot. When the 40mm round exploded, the rest of the team opened fire on the escorts who were standing and engaged in looking at the elephant as it started to run off.

    I watched a second 40mm round land behind the lumbering elephant. The rider was now screaming. What he was yelling, we did not know. But what ever he was saying, he was saying it loudly. Less than fifteen seconds had passed and the elephant had disappeared. However, we could still hear it trumpeting. Our attention was now focused on the squad of enemy soldiers. If we could silence them fast enough, we could still get the rider.

    A minute had gone by, maybe two. The escorts appeared to be down and no longer in a defensive mode. We stopped firing. The escorts were silent. The One-zero was motioning for us to move forward when we started taking fire from our flank. Large caliber and small caliber arms opened up on us. Large green tracers whizzed by overhead. RPG rounds began to explode against trees near us and behind us. Bullets cracked going by and whacked the growth around us. It didn't take long for us to realize that a larger force, a much larger force, had been following the elephant with its rider.

    The small squad of escort soldiers was forgotten. The elephant was forgotten. The dude dressed in white was forgotten. We ran. We never fired a shot towards our attackers. We continued to move away and firing behind us didn't slacken. We were hundreds of yards away before the volume of fire slowed to single rifle shots. I didn't know exactly where they were. And I don't think they saw us. They knew the general area we were in and opened fire. Their doing that probably saved our hides.

For the rest of that day we continued to move and single rifle shots were a steady reminder of what was behind us. The sun set, the moon rose and we had moonlight under the broken canopy. We continued to move. All that night and into the next morning we walked and slowly put ground between us and those we were sure were following our tracks. We moved more rapidly than normal. Not much faster, but quicker than we liked. We changed directions. We missed our contact times. We missed our meals. We missed our rest. But we were in one piece with no injuries. Mid morning came and there were no more shots behind us. We slowed down to our normal pace and moved on.

After almost 24 hours of continuous movement, we found a spot and collapsed. We rested and ate our meals. We waited for signs that we were still being chased. There weren't any. That night we made our contact time, provide our location, referenced the man on the elephant and a firefight, indicated we were safe, and asked for an extraction. The next morning we were directed to a pick up point. We gladly complied and were picked up. Six days on the ground and all we had seen was that squad of men and the elephant with the rider. I never saw any of the other soldiers who were doing their best to end our careers. I do not know for sure how many there were. But from the volume of fire, it had to be a platoon or larger.

The intel people were real interested in our elephant story. How was the rider dressed? How big was he? What was his nationality? What kind of an elephant was it? What color was it? How big were its ears? Was the rider in a chair? How large was the escort? What kind of weapons could we identify? We answered the questions as best we could. What happened to the elephant? What happened to the rider? Was he wounded by the grenade round? We didn't know!

Today I can close my eyes and still see that elephant crashing through the vegetation. The rider on top of the elephant waiving his arms and screaming as the elephant disappeared into jungle. I hope he survived. He had a good story to tell his grandchildren. Our plan was good. We just didn't know that elephant was being followed by half of the NVA in that section of Cambodia.

Had that larger group of soldiers been as closes as they were at the time we planned our ambush as they were when we executed it, we would have known they were there. They would have passed us as we planned our little adventure. Sometime during our movement to the spot of our ambush, the larger force had moved closer to the person they were guarding. Or maybe they were not part of the escort. Maybe they were a larger force that was near by and reacted to our firing upon the elephant. Maybe they were the activity in the area that we had been searching for all along. We will never know.

This was the only incident were the "do not engage the enemy rule" was broken by a team that I was on. A chance had presented itself to capture what appeared to be a high ranking individual working with the NVA. It didn't work out. But we managed to finish the mission without loss or injury to the team. And we gave the intel people something to think about!

13

AN ENEMY ATTACK

I was sound asleep. Or as sound asleep as one learns to sleep in a combat zone. In a combat zone, you sleep but the senses never totally shut down. The brain is always on the search for the sound or smell that signals danger. It was about one thirty in the morning. From off in the distance the thump of mortar rounds startled me. I jumped up from the bed, pulled on my pants, thrust my feet into my boots, and grabbed my weapon and magazine bag from a nail hanging on the wall above my bed. I screamed, "Incoming" as the first rounds were impacting somewhere in the compound near my hooch.

Busting out of the door, I ran the seventy five yards to a fighting position and jumped into the dark hole. After searching the ground between us and the artillery company, I turned around and faced towards the center of our camp. On my right was an empty foxhole. On my left was an empty bunker. The night felt cool, but sweat rolled down my face and the inside of my thighs. The hum of the generator died and the lights in our compound went out. The compound was quiet except for the thump of outgoing illumination rounds and the exploding incoming mortar and rocket rounds. I waited. Staring into the night I strained to see movement. Any movement!

Shadows of buildings raced across the ground as illumination flares drifted on their parachutes. The sweat continued to run. I felt the need to urinate but continued to hug the wall of the fighting position and stare into the night. My right thumb rubbed back and forth across the selective fire lever on the receiver of the M-16. It is a habit; it's comforting. The shadows continue to march across the ground and disappear in the darkness between the buildings. I start tapping my right foot against the bottom of the foxhole. The urge to piss grew stronger.

    The pop, pop, pop of distant small arms fire reaches me and the urge to piss fades away. Green and red tracers race across the compound and over my head. The point of the attack is at a position several hundred yards from where I stand and stare into the night. The pop, pop, pop becomes a roar as the defensive weapons open up and join the staccato of the incoming fire. Red tracers race out and away from the compound's berm. Some bounce into the air in a fiery arc. Someone is shooting too low and into the ground or the rounds are striking the posts supporting the wire obstacles that surround the camp.

    Time slows and crawls by. From the flares drifting above to the shadows crawling across the ground, everything seems to be in slow motion. It is now a waiting game and I play my part and wait. For the guys in the firefight, I know that time has stopped. Senses are being overwhelmed. Nothing exists except the tracers and human targets in front of their positions. Find the next target and engage it! For them, find the next target and engage it had become the mission.

    I strain to see into the shadows to see if any of the enemy has broken through the defensive line. Nothing moves except the shadows. The camp mortars are now firing a mixture of illumination and HE. The loud thumps of outgoing rounds momentarily drown out the sounds of small arms fire. I hear a truck start up and I follow the sound of its movement until the sound is lost in the noise of the firing weapons. Explosions outside the compound join the crescendo of those exploding inside. Suddenly the flash of a drum of exploding jellied gas brightens the night. The flames leap out and up into the sky. Black smoke boils and then the night goes dark except for the drifting flares and flashes from firing weapons. I hear the whine of a minigun and the night is lit up by hundreds, or maybe thousands of tracers. The noise lasts a second or two and the night darkens as the tracers burn out.

A new sound joins this symphony of noise, "Ka-boom, ka-boom, ka-boom". It is the sound of the artillery company's Duster tossing 40mm rounds towards the unseen hill. I watch the tracers race outward and explode against a target. I can't see it, but I know the rounds are exploding on and above the hill. The noise of small arms fire slows and then stops. The pop of illumination rounds and the ka-boom from the duster is all you hear until the 175mm guns and the 8 inch howitzers open up. They crash! They roar! And off in the distance following each round's departure comes the sound of a pop and then a multitude of small explosions. After twelve to fifteen rounds from the big guns, all is quiet except for the occasional pop from an illumination round.

For what seems like ages, there is no noise except for the sound of an occasional illumination round being fired and the hiss of the burning flares as they drift back to earth. I watch the shadows resume their race across the camp. The feeling of being in slow motion is gone. I stare into the night. Behind me I can hear the Duster move to a new location. I turn and search for the source of the noise. I can't see it, but I can follow the squeak of its tracks as it creeps slowly towards the east.

A new sound attracts my attention and I look up. The sound is an airplane slowly moving from the northeast. I can't see any lights. The sound stops moving westward and appears to be almost stationary. I realize that it is circling. Large flares pop in the area of the plane and float towards the ground. A bright line of fire reaches out from the sky and races towards the ground. The whine of a minigun reaches me at about the same time the stream of fire begins to look like a piece of burning rope falling to the ground. The stream of fire begins again, this time closer to where the hill to our north is located. Again the whine of a minigun reaches me. The bright red arc again ends in the sky and falls to earth. More flares drop and pop. Spooky, a C-47 gunship, is finishing up what ever is left of the enemy forces that attacked us.

A generator starts up. Lights come back on. The siren sounds all clear. I climb out of my hole and the urge to urinate returns. I stand and piss on the backside of the berm. The relief feels good! A voice calls out asking if I'm okay. I hear laughter and friends calling to one another from different areas of the camp. I feel tired. A look at my watch tells me that an hour and a half has passed. It seems more like three hours. During the slow walk back to my room, I clear my weapon. The loose round from the chamber is pushed back into the top of the magazine. The weapon goes back on the wall and I hit the rack.

In the morning I walked to the area where the majority of fighting had taken place. Since daylight, teams of men have been replacing wire and mines. A few dead NVA or VC soldiers are still in some sections of the wire obstacles. Some are laid out in a row on the ground waiting to be tossed into the back of a truck. Who are these half dressed men that attacked our camp? I don't know what they are. Many are almost naked. A pair of shorts and funny looking canvas and rubber shoes are all many of them are wearing. They could be soldiers from the North or insurgents from the surrounding area. It doesn't make much of a difference who or what they are. Now they are just dead men who have nothing more to give for their country or their political ideals.

Most of the men are laughing and joking as they go about their duties. A few are quiet and work like zombies. In a few weeks, this area will look like the rest of the areas surrounding the camp. The only signs that a firefight took place here will be the blackened wire and a few dented posts. The grass will grow. The dust and dirt will stain the new posts and camouflage what happened here. A friend that I play cards with tells me that the club took a hit from a rocket. Questions race through my mind as I walk back towards the club.

Why did they try it last night? How many were there? How many of the killed or wounded were carried off? How big a force will they mass next time? The S-2 says that ten to twelve percent of the locals working in the camp are VC. What was their roll in the attack? Did some of dead work in our camp or walk the roads around us in the daytime? The Vietnamese you meet during the day are so friendly and they laugh and joke at the smallest thing. How many of them are smiling at us during the day and firing weapons at us at night? Will I be here or in the woods during the next one? What happens to the teams on the ground if this compound gets overrun? At some point in this questioning, I realize there are no answers to the questions. And if someone could answer the questions, it wouldn't make any difference. What will be, will be. We have a mission to complete!

I can see the hole in the club wall well before I reach it. A blackened scar surrounds the three to four foot hole in wall on the north side of the structure. Last night there were forty to fifty men sitting on the other side of that wall and watching a movie. The show had ended about midnight. Had that rocket landed then, there would have been a large number of casualties.

I begin another day. There is a mission to get ready for. I know that I feel safer in the woods. When the compound gets hits, I feel like a bird in a cage. I hope that the cage is strong enough to stand the attack. I can't help feeling like the cage will break one day if the enemy can mass a large enough force. In the jungle there are miles and miles of cover and concealment. Here there is nothing but open terrain around me. In the jungle, the enemy doesn't know were I am. Here, they can see us from that damn hill. When the camp is attacked and I am in it, I can do nothing but sit and wait. I think that it is the waiting and inactivity that makes it so bad for me. There is nothing to do but watch the flashes of light and hang on to my weapon and thoughts. Then there is the chance that on one night; one of those first to arrive rockets or mortar rounds is going to land on a barracks. I hope I am not there when it happens.

I don't know why I felt more secure in the jungle than in the compound. Thinking about it, it really didn't make much sense. The compound was really secure. Besides the fixed defenses of a berm, wire, mines, guard towers, and such, there was also a proactive defense. Patrols from the compound went out daily and searched for signs of enemy movement around the compound. Aircraft that supported our operations often made sweeps around the compound in the early mornings and late evenings. The Mike Force that supported our operations and the local CIDG companies also made sweeps and daily patrols. It really would have been a very difficult task to assemble an enemy force large enough to overrun the camp without the allied forces in the area knowing about it. The occasional sniper attack and the rockets and mortars were inaccurate. The only real threat was the chance of sneaking in a dozen or so sappers armed with explosive charges and grenades into the camp.

A week or two later part of the attack became a joke. The night of the attack, dozens of RPG's were fired at our compound. Only two struck anything. The rest passed over the compound and exploded in the open field behind us. We could just imagine a young NVA soldier standing next to a soldier firing the RPG's at our compound and screaming, "I carried these damn things down hundreds of miles of jungle trails. I was shot at and bombed! All of that just to watch you shoot the damn things into an empty field".

Every soldier in Vietnam experienced an attack or multiple attacks on the places where they lived. No camp or compound was immune to attacks of one kind or another. If the camps did not suffer physical assaults by enemy soldiers, they at least experience rocket and mortar attacks and an occasional sniper. A number of Special Forces camps and Army Fire Bases were overrun. The camps along the border areas caught hell. But even those incidences of overrunning a camp could not be called enemy successes, the camps were back in American hands within a few days.

Attacks on camps also came from within. In many camps, the VC working inside the camps left booby traps or attempted to damage or make inoperative parts of the camp defense. This included such things as removing the explosive charges from mines and removing parts from weapon that were on a camp's perimeter. Safety and survival meant constant vigilance and the checking and rechecking of camp defenses.

14

SOME NOT SO BRIGHT IDEAS

You wonder sometimes, where some people get the ideas they do and what the reasoning is behind the idea. The following are two prime examples.

Between our compound and the city of Ban Me Thuot was a stretch of the MSR (main service route) that ran straight as an arrow for miles through the middle of a rubber tree plantation. The area was pleasing to the eye. Compared to the rest of Vietnam, it was relatively clean. Fruit and banana trees grew here and there adjacent to whitewashed buildings. The squalor and war damage was absent. This was not a free fire zone! The area was dotted with old French plantation buildings and row upon row of rubber trees.

The only draw back to traveling in this area was the occasional ambush. Local VC often took advantage of the terrain and would open up on vehicles with bursts of small arms fire. After emptying a magazine or two they would disappear into the acres and acres of rubber trees. Return fire was almost never accomplished. The VC attackers never stayed to fight. By the time a vehicle realized it was under attack and got stopped, the enemy was gone. And if you did return fire and damaged the rubber trees, you got your ass chewed, and compensation had to be paid to the owners of the trees. This was the situation into which I would one day ride.

With blue skies all the way to the horizon, the day was warm but not too hot. I was on the second day of a rest cycle. In the middle of the afternoon, seven of us decided to go to town for a seafood dinner. The only available vehicle was a 5/4 ton truck (a vehicle that looks like an oversized pick up truck). At the appointed departure hour, I climbed into the back of the vehicle and flopped down on a folding bench seat. My Browning rode comfortably tucked into the waistband of my pants in the small of my back. Two of the guys rode in the cab and four others were spread out along the bench seats with me.

The rear of the truck was now cramped. Mounted in the rear, over the wheels was a mini-gun. Two tubs of ammunition that fed the gun were against the cab of the vehicle. The bench seats mounted on each side of the bed were normally kept in the folded up position and just managed to clear the gun mounts when folded down for troops to sit on them. I didn't care about the seating condition. I had never gone to town before. I was doing something new and the breeze felt good as we drove along the MSR.

When we reached ambush alley the driver picked up speed. After traveling of some time, we pasted a newly posted speed limit sign. Our driver ignored it. As we continued on we yelled comments and jokes into the wind about the stupidity of someone posting a speed limit sign in an area were ambushes were common. As the comments were being screamed into the breeze, an American military police jeep, with two MP's on board, pulled out behind us and gave chase with their siren wailing and a red light flashing on the right front fender. Since I had been facing to the front, I had no clue from where they had appeared or for how long they had been behind us.

The driver of our vehicle started to slow down. My eyes were on the jeep racing up behind us. Out of the corner of my eye I caught the movement of a hand as it reached out and hit the triggers on the mini gun. I heard the distinctive whine of the gun. A bucket full of brass spewed into the truck bed as flames leaped from the six rapidly rotating barrels. A line of tracers raced past the tops of the MP's heads and bounced off the road hundreds of yards behind them.

The driver of the jeep slammed on the brakes. With screeching tires, the jeep made donuts on the pavement and the driver somehow managed to get stopped without an accident or injury. Our driver kept on going. We found the situation funny and laughed our asses off. Much of the talk during the rest of the trip was about the MP's soiling their pants and the jeep spinning down the roadway.

After eating and drinking a few beers, we made our way back to camp. We did not meet or see an MP vehicle on the MSR going home. When we did get back, the Sergeant Major was waiting for us. I don't think he believed the story that the firing of the mini gun was an accident. I don't know if it was an accident or not. But after a ten minute ass chewing, the only thing that happened to us was a restriction on taking that 5/4 ton into town again. The 25 MPH speed limit signs stayed up, but I don't recall any reports of MP's trying to enforce the speed limit in ambush alley after that date.

I imagine the incident scared the hell out of the MP's. I know they didn't expect anything like that to happen. In all fairness, they didn't deserve it. The individual who owned the hand that hit the switch claimed that it was an accident. He said that our vehicle hit a bump or something and he reached out to steady himself. We all accepted his claim of innocence. And we all agreed that we and the MP's were lucky that the gun was pinned so it couldn't traverse or change elevation. Most of all, we were glad that only a piece of an ammo belt was in the gun and a small number of rounds had been fired.

This roadway was the only way we had to get from our compound to the city. And the drivers of our vehicles normally drove at 50 to 60 miles an hour when traveling this section or road because of the history of attacks there. The day a 25 MPH speed limit sign showed up along this section of the MSR the situation became a joke. We couldn't believe that someone was that stupid. It did not seem possible that someone was dumb enough to place a speed limit sign in an area that was known for vehicle ambushes. It was a sign that everyone ignored. For some reason, after this incident, none of our vehicles were ever stopped again for speeding.

A few operations could go into the not so bright idea pool. The following is an example. Our team was alerted to an operation that involved a river near the border. The intel people believed that the NVA had constructed a submerged bridge and were using the bridge at night to cross troops and equipment. The bridge was believed to be six to eight inches below the surface and anchored on each side of the river bank with heavy cables. The recon team I was on was detailed to find it.

The plan, as laid out by operations, was for us to insert two days from the river; carry two rubber boats to a selected point; launch the boats at night and drift down the river and find the bridge. No one wanted to hear our thoughts on the idea; maybe because all of them were negative.

Preparation for the mission included an extra week of prep time in order to teach our indigenous scouts how to operate a three man rubber boat. After the two rubber boats arrived we spent two days inflating and deflating the boats as well as teaching hand signals and boat operations on dry land. Then we went to a small lake near a Montagnard village to practice what had been taught on dry land. After two days of practice on the water, the Yard team members could inflate, launch, and maneuver the boats fairly efficiently.

Following all the other normal preparations, the team was inserted and we started our search for the hidden bridge. Instead of two days, it took us three to reach a point near our selected river trip launch point. During this trek, the Yards carried the two pumps and the paddles. The boats were carried by the One-one and me. Must I say the damn things were heavy? Well, they weren't really all that heavy; maybe 18 to 20 pounds apiece. However, their weight added to my normal load made my rucksack seem quite heavy. And they felt awkward lashed to the bottom of my pack. Anyway, on the morning of the third day we were told to forget the boats and move to a designated point and confirm the position of the bridge. So before moving out that morning, we slashed the rubber boats, buried the pumps and paddles, and moved out on our new mission.

Before we committed that foolish act of floating on the river, someone with some rank finally realized that it probably wasn't smart to have people drifting down to a bridge during the time it was believed to be heavily used. I can still picture us trying to drift across a bridge while it was being used by a large number of armed enemy soldiers. The thought of would could have been isn't pretty.

Anyway, we went to the indicated point. We didn't find any enemy soldiers. But we did find the anchor points for the underwater bridge and noted their position. We were extracted and the next day the bridge was bombed. I still can't believe that I carried a three man rubber boat for three days in the jungle and then threw it away without using it. Our recon team may have become to only assault boat trained team in the Central Highlands.

This story can be topped by another one. One day, in a pre-mission briefing, the Operations Officer presented several cans of what he called an improved mace spray. He informed us that the brains at Op 35 had determined that enemy soldiers could be captured very easily by stepping out onto a trail and spraying this improved mace spray into their face. The mace, he said, would cause so much discomfort that the enemy soldiers would be stunned, docile, and not use their weapons. My team leader asked the S3 if he would step out onto a trail and spray a man, who was armed, in the face with mace. The S-3 stated that he didn't think he would. That was as far as our use of mace went. Months later I saw several cans of the stuff in the supply room. It was there, on a shelf, along with the crossbows, tomahawks, and other equipment none of the teams would use.

Stupid ideas were compounded by the fact that some of what we reported was not believed. On one operation the One-zero reported hearing tanks on a trail. The all wise intel people didn't believe him. They said that the trail network in that area was too rough to operate tanks there. The One-zero asked to be reinserted into the same area. In a couple of weeks that happened. This time when he was extracted he brought out parts to a soviet tank, a PT-76 light amphibious tank. Then they believe him. You train someone, spend tons of money to have him report what he finds, and then you disregard what he says from the comfort of a desk chair. Didn't make sense to me!

There were some policies that also didn't make any sense. The first was free fire zone and no fire zones. In some areas you could shoot at anything that moved. In other areas you could not fire on a target unless you had clearance from above. The roadway located northeast of our compound was a no fire zone during daylight hours and became a free fire zone after dark. No one could ever give me a rational reason for this policy.

There was another policy that was crazy. You could go off to a major city but you couldn't take your weapon with you. In a country were an insurgency was taking place and you were subject to be shot at by the VC at any time or place; the no weapons policy just did not make any sense to me. I was told that the command was afraid of a racial fight taking place when soldiers from different units were drinking. That didn't make any sense either. The weapons policy was violated by Special Forces personnel. I don't know of very many that didn't go to Saigon or other towns without a handgun tucked away in their waistband.

There was an engineer compound not too far from our compound. The soldiers in that compound could not keep ammunition for their weapons with them. The ammunition was stored in connex containers and issued as necessary for those on guard or going on patrols. If the camp was attacked, everyone rushed to the connex containers and got ammunition before running to their fighting positions. That damn sure doesn't make sense!

15

THE ENEMY COULD BE STUPID TOO

Adjacent to the MSR near the town of Ban Me Thuot was a refueling point for our helicopter support. The area was a football sized field of grass. Aircraft would set down and fuel was obtained from two large rubber fuel cells. Across the MSR and adjacent to this field was a small pink block building and a cluster of other building. The pink building was about 10 by 20 feet in size with a large glass windows and a single door. The building at one time was a service station where the locals obtained gas and oil for their motor cycles and motorized carts.

One day a slick and a gun ship set down to refuel. As the slick was taking on fuel, a single gunman began firing an AK at the two aircraft. Within seconds of being fired upon, the gunship, sitting on the ground behind the slick, lifted a few feet into the air, swung its nose towards the small pink building and fired a long burst from its mini guns. The door gunner on the slick opened up with his machinegun and added to the hundreds of bullets already striking the small structure. The building was chewed up. It ceased to be a gas station or a position from which to attack refueling aircraft. At least this is the story told to me by a 20th SOS crewman as we refueled there after an operation.

I didn't at the time, and I do not today, understand the thinking and logic of such an incident. What did that one man think he was going to accomplish? One AK-47 was no match for a gunship. David had a better chance with his slingshot against the giant Goliath than this one gunman had against his intended target. But men do such things!

The incident reflects the mentality of the VC and NVA. The NVA suffered terrible losses moving south along the trail networks. They endured B-52 strikes, ordinance dropped by fast and slow movers, and attacks by gunships; first by "spooky" and then "super spook". In South Vietnam, the VC cadre was systematically being eliminated by operations and programs targeting them. I wonder at the indoctrination and the motivation of the political cadre that compelled men and women to endure so much. Were their beliefs that strong in communism? Was it the rejoining of north and south? Or was it the removal of outsiders; the French and then the Americans? We were fighting to keep communism out of other Asian countries. What were they fighting for?

Ground attacks against our compound and many others were stupid and a waste of men. Out of the hundreds of camps in Vietnam, the enemy overran a handful of them. And of those that were overrun, within a day or two, the camps were back in American hands. The losses suffered to achieve these minor victories seemed way out of balance to me.

On one recon operation, the team I was on walked into an ambush. An NVA soldier stepped on onto a trail we were crossing and yelled in Vietnamese. The point man dropped to his knees and emptied his magazine in the direction of the NVA officer. Before his magazine was empty, the rest of the team was firing into their respective sectors that we practiced on immediate action drills. Within seconds of his officer's actions, we were running for the safety of a different part of Cambodia.

After running for a hundred yards or so, we stopped to rest and listen. Before moving out in a new direction, I asked the mercenary team leader what the NVA officer had yelled. I was told that he said, "Drop your rifles and you will not be killed." I do not know how large a force was there. But I do know that if they had fired on us first, some of us would have been killed or wounded. In this incident we were able to break contact and continue the mission. I don't know the size of the enemy force that challenged us that day. I don't know how many we killed or wounded. I think the point man eliminated the NVA officer. And we got away without injuries.

I didn't understand the reasoning of the NVA officer that warned us of their presence. Why did he show himself? He could have yelled the same thing from behind a tree or from a position on the ground. He didn't. He did something stupid. And I think he died for it. Just like the shooter in the little service station.

16

STRANGERS IN THE WOODS

The flight was a long one, over an hour from our compound to our LZ. It was one of the few times we launched directly from our own compound. As we flew along at about three thousand feet, I watched the ground change from dark blotchy jungle to dark brown earth marked with bomb and artillery craters. The sun was just a glow on the horizon. As it started to climb, more and more detail became visible. The dark blotchy terrain slowly changed to dark and bright shades of green. Here and there a stream made its way to the river. Free fire zones displayed their pock marked terrain. Occasionally a large wooden and stone building, with manicured grounds would pop into view giving evidence that this was once a French vacation land.

About twenty minutes out from the LZ, the four choppers in our flight, changed their straight and level flight by dropping down to tree top level and starting their twisting and turning dance across the tops of the trees. The casual watching of the country side below changed to searching for trails and people. At this level, a brief glance is all one got of anything on the ground. The search took my mind off the tree tops and branches that flashed by just feet from the choppers skids. As we got close to the LZ, the door gunner stuck his index finger in my face and yelled, "One minute out".

I watched the trees below turn to dusty yellow and light green grass. We were over the edge of the landing zone. The slick settled towards the earth, the whine of its engine and the wop-wop of the blades was deafening. A tap on my right shoulder sent me leaping towards the ground. My feet hit something solid. I fell forward and rolled onto my side. The helicopter was a good five feet off the ground. The blast from the rotor blades kicked up dirt and pieces of grass. I shut my eyes. We were in chest high elephant grass.

For a short second or two, I lay without moving and waited the Huey lift into the air. The engine noises died away. I rolled over and got up on my knees and sat on my heels. A glance at the sun coming up over the tree line gave me my basic direction of travel. I twisted around on the balls of my feet until the sun was over my right shoulder. Comfortable now, I quit moving and concentrated on listening. Phillip, my One-one, moved and I reached out to quiet him down. After three or four minutes, I nodded to my Yard team leader. He started to stand and then dropped back down. In hand signals, he relayed that he saw men in the wood line to our front.

I eased upward until I could see above the grass. I saw an individual in a brownish green uniform. I ducked back down and waited for the firefight to start. Nothing happened. I eased up and took a longer look around. I saw several men in uniforms and one individual standing out in the open. The bright morning sun lit up the wood line illuminating areas under the tree canopy. His arms were folded across his chest and he appeared to be unarmed. I ducked back down and took the handset from Phillip.

Normal procedure was to break squelch twice to let the air assets know everything was alright. You did this by pressing the talk key twice on the hand mike without saying anything. This time I made voice contact with our support, "Tool box this is Nail, we have company."

I was asked if any shots had been fired. I told the boss, no. The next voice on the radio I heard was the FAC. He told me that the gun ships were on their way back to our location and asked what our situation was. I told him that I had seen company in about a sixty degree arc around the wood line. He asked if we were surrounded and I told him I didn't know. I stood up for a third time and looked all the way around the clearing. The bright sun to the east helped hide anything or anyone who was to our sides and behind us. I informed the FAC that I could only see company on the one side of the clearing.

The next word on the radio was that the ships were one minute out. We could now hear the approaching aircraft. From out of the sun, a gunship came in fast and low. It crossed the clearing and disappeared to the west. The FAC asked if any shots were fired. I replied in the negative. A gun ship came in again. This time it approached from the north. It crossed the clearing below tree top level and disappeared behind the tree tops to the south. Following this pass, I could hear it off in the distance. Again came the question of shots fired and I gave the same answer. I stood up and looked out over the grass. I was a target for anyone who wanted to take a shot. The man with the folder arms had disappeared. I told the FAC that I could no longer see our company, but I was sure they were still there.

The gun ships returned. This time the two of them flew across the cleaning, One from the north and the other from the east. They continued to orbit our position while flying in a tight figure eight pattern. With each pass the approach and departure directions changed. Several minutes went by as the gunships made passes above the clearing. "Slick coming in," came from the handset. Within seconds the slick came in low and settled down near us. The team raced for the helicopter and dove in. As we were lifting off I heard the door gunner screaming, No shots fired, no shots fired." It was a quiet ride back to the landing pad at Duc Lap.

Our aircraft sat down. And the XO meet the team as we got off the aircraft. He told Phillip and me to follow him. We were taken to an area off to the side of the landing strip. Phillip was led away by a senior NCO. The XO started asking me questions. What had I seen? How many individuals had I seen? How far away were they? Were we surrounded? What kind of weapons had I seen? What was the color of the clothing on these enemy soldiers?

I answered the questions as best as I could and the XO departed. In a little while Phillip came back. He couldn't tell them anything. His head had always been below the top of the thick grass. He hadn't seen anything. After about an hour, our Yard team members walked over to where Phillip and I were. The yard team leader made the comment that he thought his debriefer didn't believe him. I told him not to worry about it.

Soon after the return of the Yards, the XO returned. He informed Phillip and me that the commander wasn't very happy. He thought we should have tried to make a break from the clearing since no shots had been exchanged. He then said that the only thing that had saved our asses was the fact that some of the chopper crews also reported seeing people in the wood line. I made some remark that I was sorry that the CO was pissed, but it was my responsibility to make decisions on the ground and it was our asses out there that could get shot up and not the CO's.

The XO frowned but didn't say anything. He then informed us that we would be reinserted on our alternate LZ at dusk. My comment was close to "whatever." I was disappointed, angry, and hurt that my commander did not immediately believe the story of our having company in the wood line. And I was angry at myself for not taking any photographs. I had a camera in the outside pocket of my rucksack.

An hour or so before it got dark; we loaded up and took another shot at getting into our area. The insert went smoothly. We moved about two hundred yards from our LZ and settled in for the night. For the next five days we moved around in our box and saw nothing. On the sixth day we headed back towards our original insert point. When we got close, we slowed our pace to a crawl. Snails moved faster than we did. Slowly we worked our way around the wood line of the clearing. Nothing! We found nothing. No fighting positions. No bunkers. No sign that anyone had camped there. The next day we called for an extraction and were lifted out.

After our debriefing the S-3 told us that there had been much talk about who or what we had seen on our initial insert. He apologized for the commander's initial reaction to the situation and went on to suggest that it could have been a Cambodian military unit that didn't want us in the area. It could have been an NVA unit that had someone very important with them and didn't want a firefight that could get that important someone killed or injured. That was the first time anything like that had happened. No other team had reported company on the ground at the time of an insert without shots being fired.

I left the figuring out the "who and the why" to the intel people. I was just glad that we had gone in on an occupied LZ and had come out alive. That was one fear that many teams had. Other teams had dropped in on LZ's that were occupied by or surrounded by NVA units. Two teams had dropped in on what were NVA base camps with bunkers dug in around the clearings. These teams had been shot up. I felt lucky.

However, the feeling of being lucky didn't square it with the commander for me. On a previous operation where I was the One-one, our team was chased for several days after a fire fight. Several times during those three days, the One-zero asked for an extraction and the request was answered with a command to continue the operation. That was the only time I ever felt the need to use the pills (speed) that were in our survival kits. When we returned, the One-zero went to the commander's office and told him something to the effect that he had better not be left hanging out in a situation like that again. It was a threat but the commander never did anything about it.

Throughout this book, I have refrained from using people's names. Since I mentioned Phillip I will say this about him. Phillip was the only person I ever knew that was in the Phoenix program. He became ill on one of our operations. He tried his best to keep going and not cause an aborted mission. By the third day, he was too ill to carry the weight of his equipment and I called for an extraction. After we were extracted, he went to the field hospital at Cam Rahn Bay. About three weeks later he returned. A few days later he came to my room and said good-by. During our short talk he told me that he had requested a transfer to Phoenix and showed me his assignment orders. He also showed me blanket travel orders and a brand new suppressed .32 caliber Berretta. That was the last I saw of Phillip. I hope life treated him well.

17

HOW CLOSE CAN YOU GET?

The insertion was quick and clean. With the sun popping up on the horizon, we dropped in west of a suspected high speed trail that was the focus of the mission. The location had been targeted by a FAC spotting smoke coming from double canopy jungle. By our plan we had two days to reach the specific area Ops wanted us to search. We figured that we would be near the trail by late afternoon of the second day or early morning of the third. The slow methodical pace of the first day took us through double canopy forest with head high and taller undergrowth growing on undulating ground. During some ten hours of walking, we saw and crossed nothing of interest but two small streams.
    When it became too dark to travel, we just circled up for the night. The ground cover was that thick. The heavy growth was like a security blanket. The One-Zero encoded his message for the final daily contact. We ate a meal while waiting for our contact time. After sending our message, we buried our trash, pulled a poncho liner out of our rucksacks and settled down for the night. Our only concern was to keep watch on our back trail. We felt that if trouble was to come during the night, it would come from that direction.
    Dawn came. I ate a light breakfast of plain rice. We sent our morning message detailing our location, situation, and direction of travel and moved out. About midmorning the terrain changed to single canopy on rolling ground with patches of waist to chest high fern like plants among four foot tall ant and termite mounds. Sunlight found gaps in the high canopy and caused a light and dark patchwork across the ground and

vegetation. We slowed our pace. Walk a little and then stop, look, and listen. Walk some more and then stop, look, and listen. Yesterday you couldn't see more than 30 yards. Now you could see for a hundred yards or so.

    We made contact. Unexpected contact! I heard a voice yell something in Vietnamese. Then I heard firing. I knew it was the point man firing his weapon. The One-Zero screamed, "One eighty, one eighty" as he too emptied his weapon. I brought my weapon up and emptied the magazine into the vegetation to my front and right flank. I could hear the Yards behind me emptying their weapons as I turned to run back the way we had come. The thud of the M79 being fired registered. The sound of the exploding grenade round caught up with me as I raced back down the track we had just made.

    The One Zero passed me in his dash to get back in front of me and take command. He stopped the flight and returned the teams' bolt for safety to a fast walk and then a halt to review the situation. We had just walked into an ambush. Was it for us or someone else? Was there a blocking force behind us? Sounds came from the direction of the recent contact. A single gunshot was answered by three shots on our left flank. The One-zero pulled a claymore mine off my ruck, set it down facing the way we had come, pulled the fuse igniter and we moved out at a fast walk.

    About four and a half minutes later we heard the explosion behind us. A few seconds later a gunshot sounded on our left flank. It was answered by two shots behind us. We turned north and slowed down. The One-Zero got on the radio and requested an extraction. Break contact and continue was the answer. The One-Zero requested the extraction for a second time. The answer was the same, "break contact and continue the mission." At a quick pace we traveled north for about two clicks. We then turned east and resumed our routine of walk a short distance and then stop, look and listen.

    After a couple of peaceful hours we turned south. We were now on a course that took us back towards the area of the ambush. Signal shots continued to be fired west and north of us. It was now late afternoon and darkness wasn't far off. The sunlight in the high tree tops indicated that the sun was sinking and we were not sure of out situation. Had we really broken contact? There was no circling back to check on our trail. If trackers were there, they would have to stop when the sun went down the same way we would.

At the last fading light, we found a clump of trees and settled in between them. The light faded and the night surrounded us. I felt almost safe. There was a lot of jungle to hide in. Too much ground for the enemy to effectively search in such a shot period of time. Surly nothing would happen during the night.

The One-zero prepared a message and we made our scheduled contact. We were eating when someone fired a rifle. The shot was not more than five or six hundred meters away. The shot came from our northwest. It was answered by a shot from the southwest. Eating was forgotten. The enemy was not far away.

From the direction of the first shot, voices could now be heard. The interpreter leaned in close to the One-zero and whispered something. The One-zero leaned towards me and whispered, "They are keeping soldiers on line and they are saying to take the American's alive". I looked around. It was black. I felt more than saw the One-zero's presence near me. I looked up. We were below a section of scattered canopy. I could see stars. Where was the moon? If it came up, how much illumination would creep into our hiding place?

A new sound reached my ears. People, soldiers, were beating on things. Faintly and then ever more distinctly, the sounds increased in volume. Like an ocean wave the noise swept towards us from the northwest. I thought of an English fox hunt. I could picture the English hunters dressed in red and waiting for the fox to be chased towards them by a long line of peasants blowing horns, yelling, and singing. Only we were not foxes and we were not going to run. We had a better chance of avoiding contact by using the night and staying still.

The noise continued its steady movement towards us. The banging of wood on wood, wood on metal, and metal on metal steadily grew louder. My One-zero broke the silence and whispered, "What ever happens, do not run. That's what they want you to do. We will fight them if we have to, but not the way they want it. And don't do anything unless I do something first!" As quietly as I could, I tucked my AK in next to my body and removed two grenades from my load bearing harness. I laid one of the grenades, a fragmentation grenade, on the ground almost under my chin. The other, a big fat white phosphorus grenade, I held in my right hand. The thought that I did not want to be captured entered my mind. I had an AK magazine in my right leg pocket with the doctored rounds in it and a 61mm mortar round in my rucksack!

The noises grew in volume. In addition to the banging of objects together, I could now hear the snapping of branches and individuals talking in Vietnamese. I folded my arms, stuck my hands under my armpits, and rested my head against my forearms. The heavy grenade was a reassuring lump in my hand. At one point I could hear foot steps, the rustling of vegetation on the ground by slow plodding feet. I think I stopped breathing. I slightly turned my head to the side and searched for the noise.

I saw nothing! There was only blackness. Then I realized I could no longer see the night sky. My vision of the stars was blocked by the head and shoulder of a soldier walking by. I felt the hair on my arms and the back of my neck rise up. Slowly the sight of the stars returned and the noises continued on. Normal breathing returned. The banging and voices grew fainter and fainter. An occasional gun shot was still fired here and there. But they were all well to our south and southwest.

I felt a rush. I felt hot and then cold. My clothing was damp with sweat. My One-zero's hand momentarily touched my side and withdrew. After a while there was silence. It was over. Our space belonged only to us. The enemy soldiers had walked right by us. I hung the two grenades on my load bearing harness.

I tried to figure out how close they had come. Four feet? Five feet? Ten feet? No farther away than ten feet! They had walked around our clump of trees and vegetation. How many had there been? Twenty? Thirty? Fifty? I don't know. How could they not have seen us? How could they not have smelled us? I felt tired. Exhausted! The incident had been one hell of an adrenalin rush. I fell asleep looking at the stars.

The next morning we made our scheduled contact, ate breakfast, and moved out. Still moving south, we passed the area of our initial contact and turned west towards our objective. The rest of the operation was pretty much routine. The trail turned out to be a slow speed trail, a foot and bike path. After watching it for two days and only seeing civilian traffic, we dropped the Italian Green, moved to our primary pick up point and were extracted.

Making contact with an enemy force was one of the hazards of the job. During one operation, I ran down a high speed trail with a gunship overhead. Brass from fired rounds rained down around the team and I as we moved as quickly as we could towards a pick up point. It was the only time I walked or ran on a high speed trail. And even though there was a large enemy force chasing us and shooting in our direction, it was daylight and we had the gunships with us. I knew we would get out. No other operation was as precarious for me as that one where I came close to being stepped on by an enemy soldier.

I don't remember exactly how many recon operations I took part in; but on three of them the recon team made unexpected contacts and a fire fight ensued. On two of those occasions it was over in less than two minutes and we had miles of jungle to disappear into. On one incident, the fight lasted for some twenty minutes before we were able to get away. As far as combat goes, I was fortunate. Most of the inserts I made ended up being dry holes; no enemy and no contact.

That one night of sitting and waiting and hearing the NVA move towards us was the worse situation that I experienced. It was far worse than being in a fire fight. It took a couple of hours for those NVA soldiers to reach our location and move past us. There was nothing to do but lie there in the dark and wait for them to come. There was nothing to do but spend time thinking of all the things that could happen and prepare myself to make their life as miserable as possible if they found us.

I can't say that this sort of incident happened to recon teams on a regular bases. But it did happen enough that it was not uncommon. The fact is that other teams experienced much more dangerous situations than my example. Most managed to slip away.

Somewhere I read that less than a thousand men were assigned to SOG teams throughout the six years of SOG's existence. About 300 SOG members or one third of the force were lost, killed, or missing. No SOG team members were released when American POW's came home from North Vietnam.

18

THE LLDB

I never worked with ARVN soldiers and I don't know very much about the South Vietnamese Special Forces (the LLDB). I know they were used extensively in the operations run by Delta. I know that they were not under the command of the South Vietnamese Army. The South Vietnamese government created a secret command in 1958. This command was designated the Vietnamese Special Forces Command in 1963. The soldiers in this command were directly under the control of the President of South Vietnam. So they did pretty much what they wanted to.

There were twelve to fifteen LLDB soldiers in our compound. Four or five were officers and the rest were enlisted men. You would think that they would have been running operations with us. I don't recall that ever happening. I can't think of any operation where an American led team went on an operation with one of our Vietnamese Special Forces counterparts. I only recall two or three times where I saw LLDB soldiers with a weapon and rucksack. I do know that they did conduct operations. What they were or where they took place is a mystery to me. My gut feeling is that they were as good a soldier as you would find anywhere else and they wanted a democratic government.

The central highlands and the mountains that I could see in the distance were supposed to be NVA strongholds. They were the hiding place of the sappers and assault troops that attacked our compound and other units in the area. These mountains may have been the areas where our Vietnamese Special Forces counterparts conducted their operations.

I remember one night in the club when I was asked if I remembered a certain LLDB soldier. I said yes. And then I was told that he had gone out on an operation with an LLDB team and did not come back. The point of the story ended up being that someone thought he was a double agent and the LLDB took him out into the bush and eliminated him. That story fit in with hearing that their main function was to eliminate the VC in the area.

On another occasion our team came back from an operation and we found a wire cage had been erected near the center of the compound. The cage was about five feet long, three feet high, and three feet wide. Inside the cage was a female dressed in the typical black pajama dress. The LLDB would go out and urinate on the female, scream at her and laugh. I was told that she was a prisoner and that the LLDB had captured on one of their patrols. Two days later she was gone along with the temporary cage. I never did find out the who, what, or why of the story. If any of us felt she was being mistreated, we had no control in any of it. She was a prisoner of the South Vietnamese Army on South Vietnamese property. I and others had some second thoughts about things that happened under the control of South Vietnams government and military forces. However, you can only do so much to influence a foreign government that thinks of things in a light much different than you see things in.

Now that I think of it, I can't recall any of our team members spending any time with the Vietnamese LLDB. It was like we lived in our world and they lived in theirs. It was a strange way to operate an alliance.

Since I brought up the female VC, if that in fact was what she was, I would like to take a moment and comment on female soldiers. There were female soldiers with the VC and the NVA. They fought just as hard as the men. Most were support troops that manned antiaircraft guns, provided security along the trail networks, and ran the radio nets. A few though, were rock hard combat soldiers that faced American firepower as well as the men did.

Later in my military career, I would hear my fellow soldiers talking about how females don't belong in the Army. How they can't take the stress of combat or they were too weak to carry their load. I think back to a female supply sergeant I served with in the U.S. at Fort Stewart, Georgia. She prepared for and passed an IG inspection and then went to the hospital and delivered a baby thirty minutes later.

When I think about the female VC and NVA soldiers in Vietnam and the American female soldiers I served with in the United States and overseas, I'm confident that the average well trained female soldier will do as well as the average well trained male in most military jobs.

19

WHAT I REMEMBER
And what I learned

      War isn't continuous combat. Soldiers spend days sitting and waiting and hours patrolling with no contact. And then a few hours or a day with soldiers in a firefight. Out of all the operations I went on, only sections of a handful stand out in my memories as having been really dangerous. The rest are just jumbled up together in a series of inserts, walks through rough terrain, and extractions. The operations are not really what I remember the most. The pickup volleyball and basketball games (they didn't happen that often), the all day long card games (there were a number of them), and the trips outside the camp seem easier to remember.
      There were invitations to a Rhade villages and the consumption of rice wine. The wine was in a large clay pot. You drank the stuff by sucking on a bamboo straw. As you drank, a village elder would pour water back into the pot. The lumps and soft stuff you sucked up with the liquid were just swallowed. While drinking the stuff, you wondered if the lumps were rice grains, worms, or something else? I had no desire to learn what the lumps were. I had no desire to look like a wimp to my American or Rhade friends so I, along with others, drank the stuff. An invite to the village meant you had been accepted by the Rhade people and to be invited was an honor. On your first visit you usually got the bowl of rice with a chicken head in it. Ever eat a meal with a chicken head staring at you? It can be loads of laughs; especially so when you are full of rice wine.

During stand downs or rest breaks, you could go to Saigon. If that didn't suit you, you could hop on a blackbird and end up in Thailand or Hong Kong. Some guys went to Australia. When we worked, we worked hard. When we played, we did it with gusto. Being able to catch a ride on one of the U.S. Air Force Special Operations blackbird flights were a benefit of being in SOG. All of the special operations people looked out for each other no matter what branch of the services you were in. It wasn't hard to arrange travel to far off places. Thinking of Saigon makes me think of a particular soldier. He carried a pair of handcuffs. He used to say that the only use they got was handcuffing an "all night girl" to his wrist so she couldn't sneak off during the night with his clothes, ID card, or money.

We liked the indigenous people we worked with. We liked the South Vietnamese. We didn't like or dislike the North Vietnamese. Sure, there were derogatory remarks made. We called them, the North Vietnamese, names like rice burners and slopes. But as far as there being any hate or emotion involved, I didn't see any. I didn't feel any. We had a job to do. We understood what they were trying to do. It was kind of like two fighters entering a boxing ring. They punched. We punched back. And that was that. The war and the operations stayed on a professional level and personal feeling pretty much stayed out of the way. When someone was lost or killed, we got angry. But the anger and feeling were directed at the situation and not the people. Letting things get personal got in the way of doing the job.

By now you should have realized that I was a member of Recon Team Nail. The indigenous team leader and interpreter was a Rhade Montagnard. He was also a Colonel in FULRO (United Front for the Liberation of Oppressed Races). The motto of Special Forces is "Liberate the Oppressed". Little wonder we got along well with the Montagnards. He used to say, "Americans number one; Vietnamese number ten; North Vietnamese number fucking ten." There were times in between recon operations when we would sit on the compound's berm and talk. We talked about Vietnam, the war, and even about some American history. I was surprised at his knowledge. He wanted the Vietnamese to see and treat him as an equal.

His story as a minority wasn't much different from minorities in the United States or in other parts of the world. In addition to being seen as an equal, he wanted the Vietnamese to stop taking the Montagnards' land. He also wanted the grenades left over at the end of each operation to add to the Rhade's arms cache. He was sure that when the Americans left Vietnam, they would have to fight the Vietnamese to gain their respect and recognition. We always gave him the grenades.

I also gave him a watch. It was a self winding Omega that I had I had owned for years. It took me a few weeks to realize that something had changed after giving him the gift. On an operation, when I went to sleep, our tail gunner Y Lon was watching over me. When I was awake, he was awake and near by. I don't know when he slept. When the camp got attacked, Y Lon appeared near my fighting position. Y Lon had become my body guard. A small act of kindness on my part was repaid in a measure that far out valued the value of the watch.

At the start of this book, I stated that living in our compound was almost comfortable. It was for the most part. However, I remember trying to go to sleep during some nights and the sweat would pour off of me and run in little streams that soaked my sheets and mattress. The air seems so hot and humid it felt like trying to sleep in a steam bath. There weren't really many nights like that. But they were so intense in discomfort that it seemed like they happened more than they did. These nights were the worst of camp life. And to me, worse than the occasional shelling or enemy attack. The attacks lasted for an hour or two. The heat and humidity stayed.

Was there a downside to serving in Vietnam? There was for some. For most there was the fact of being so far from family and friends. There was the feeling of loss and anger when a team or team member did not come back from an operation. And then there was Jerry. Jerry wasn't on a recon team but he stayed in the same barracks we did. He had earned the right to. Jerry has spent several years in Vietnam. He was on his third or forth straight year in country when I met him.

During his years there he had been with the CIDG program, ran several recon teams, and was at the time in charge of a Mike Force platoon. Jerry had a shoe box full of medals, a ton of friends, and his room was next to mine.

But Jerry drank way too much and on many nights he cried himself to sleep. And the sleep he found often contained nightmares. Whatever the ghosts were that tormented his nights, he kept them to himself. He also kept to himself the problems or motivation that kept him in county. In every way one can think of, Jerry was everything a Special Forces soldier could be or wanted to be. Brave, dedicated, and good natured, he died leading his platoon against a much larger NVA force. His death occurred while I was out on an operation. Jerry's name was the only name I searched for when I visited the Vietnam Memorial in Washington.

Did my service in Vietnam have an affect on me? Yes it did. An outward effect is that I started wearing a Rolex watch, the GMT model, during that tour and I still wear a Rolex today. An emotional effect was my loss in the pleasure of hunting. Prior to going to Vietnam, I was an avid hunter. Duck and deer hunts were something that I enjoyed. I stopped hunting when I came back from my Vietnam experience. The killing of anything had a new perspective. I have no problems with those who hunt strictly for the food. I do have an issue with the promoting of hunting as a sport. Baiting a field and then shoot a deer from a hundred yards away with a 7mm Remington is not what I call sporting. And that is how most hunters hunt these days. The tour also changed how I see the world in regards to our government, humanity, social issues, our living standards, work habits, and my view of the military. They say that it takes a significant emotional event to change people. War is such an event.

Between our gate and the airfield was a section of homes that resembled a squatter's camp. Homes were made of whatever was available. Many were made from a combination of discarded wooden packing crates, cardboard boxes, plastic sheets, sheets of tin, bamboo and timbers from the local trees. Here and there a small pathetic garden struggled to survive in the hard packed rust colored ground. Water was hauled to the homes in plastic pails and jugs. Some of these people worked in our compound or in other compounds in the area. Most earned a living by scavenging the trash dumps outside the camps for discarded rations, metal, clothing, and the other items Americans threw away.

The large cities and major towns looked like most cities in Europe. There were broad well lit streets filled with cars, motorcycles, and bikes. Stores, restaurants, bars, and whore houses lined the streets. In the country, the houses and building were smaller and not as well kept. Most of the people outside the cities lived in bamboo and grass structures. The farmers struggled daily to raise a pig or two, keep a few chickens, and grow rice and other crops. Sanitation standards were almost nonexistent. We used to say that the people in the country probably didn't care what kind of government they had; that they just wanted to be left alone to grow their rice and raise their kids.

The thought registered with me while I was there that most Americans do not realize just how well they live compared to people in other areas of the world. Our poor live better than most people do in the rest of the world. On drives through the mountains of West Virginia and the poor sections of major cities, I never saw the hunger and the needs I saw outside our compound. I believe that picture became another reason to fight because I could not believe that South Vietnam would ever be better under the rule of the Communist North.

We live in an open society. We enjoy freedoms that many around the world do not enjoy. But I believe that there has to be some things that our government keeps from us. We used to sit in the club and hear news casts of our government making statements that there wasn't any US soldiers operating in Cambodia. We laughed and thought it funny. There are bad people and governments in the world. Not everyone wishes us well. Our government needs the ability to act in secret to deal with the issues that arise from this ill will. We will always need soldiers who are willing to walk on the dark side and eliminate the most menacing of the threats against us.

One of the things I remember most was the initial smell and weight of my load bearing equipment. I can close my eyes and think of slipping into that harness and it is almost enough to gag me. Wear the same pair of sox and running shoes for a month. Exercise and get sweaty every day you wear them. Toss them in a locker for a week and then come back and see what they smell like. If they have developed a strong ammonia and stale sweat smell, you might then have an idea of the odor that assaulted my nose each time I got ready for an operation.

I remember the dust. The reddish brown dust stained everything. It was everywhere. The ground inside the camp was so compacted that very little grass grew anywhere. In the summer dust from that bare earth stained the buildings, equipment, and clothing. In the winter or wet seasons, the hard packed ground turned to mud. It was a thick mud that glued your boots to the ground. Mud and dust defined the seasons.

I remember how good a cold beer tasted after spending six or seven days eating cold meals and drinking the water from streams or bomb craters. At the end of a mission, I wasn't looking forward to a hot meal or a soft bed. The first thing I wanted was a cold beer and the second was a hot shower and clean clothes. If you want to know why, wear your clothes, the same clothes day and night for a week. Run in them. Work in them. Get good and sweaty every day. Then you will understand the desire for a cold drink, a hot shower, and clean clothes

Most Americans have never really seen the night sky as it should be seen. I never realized the amount of stars and how clear and bright the night sky was until I viewed it from the dark jungle floor. Having grown up around military bases and cities, I never really got to see the night sky. The brightness and the quantity of stars seen from a dark place with clean air are amazing. I would not see it that way again until I saw it from my boat cruising miles off the Georgia coast.

I mentioned that insertion by CH34 helicopters scared the hell out of me. I will always remember sitting in the door of a CH34 and hearing some crew member shout, "We go in now!" When the words were shouted, the helicopter was in level flight. I swear the pilot rolled that chopper over on its side and let it drop like a rock. The helicopter was no longer flying. The lift was gone. If I hadn't had a sling on my weapon and the sling around my neck, I think my weapon would have been lost.

One minute I was sitting in the doorway and looking out across the tops of the jungle and the horizon. The next second I was facing the jungle below me. I couldn't see the horizon! All I could see were the tops of trees rushing up to meet me. The aircraft was falling like a rock. I felt like I was going to fall out of the doorway. I turned loose of my weapon and grabbed on with both hands. The ground continued to rapidly advance towards me.

About 60 feet off the ground, I heard the blades start making a racket. I looked up and they were severely bent. I swear the blades looked like they were going to break, but they didn't. The chopper swung below them and returned to a level flight. Seconds later the aircraft hovered about six feet off the ground. Under my breath I cussed the tactic. I hated those inserts!

The inserts in those CH34's were the only times I think I was really afraid. Yes there were times of apprehension. There were a couple of times when I thought this was going to be the end of everything for me. But there was no fear there; only acceptance of the situation and what I must do to keep moving on. Helicopters are not flying when they are on their side and loosing altitude. And the thought of crashing in one of those birds scared me.

When it comes to achieving victory or success, there is no substitute for planning and immediate action drills. The one who is the quickest and places the most fire on a target or area is the winner. On three occasions the team I was on made unexpected close contact with a larger enemy force. In all three instances, our team was able to engage the enemy with a high volume of suppressive fire and then disengage.

In all three situations, our team was able to disengage and get away without any serious injuries. The only way we were able to accomplish this was through the constant practice of immediate action drills and then executing the practiced maneuvers when the situation called for it. If you want an operation to work, plan and practice. When bullets are flying is not the time when you want to spend a lot of time figuring out what your next move should be.

Believe it or not, it is often difficult to get an enemy soldier's attention. In a firefight, the sounds of weapons firing and exploding fragmentation grenades are just noise. It is noise that you tend to ignore. Tracers can get your attention. Our tracers were red. Theirs were green and sometimes red. Tracer rounds are something you can see and your instinct says they are something to get away from. But they don't put the fear of God into you.

In my second firefight, I learned that if you want to get the enemies attention, it has to be with something the enemy could see. It had to be something that took advantage of a natural fear. There was something they could see, really see! That something was white phosphorus! My team leader tossed a white phosphorus grenade to break contact. When it exploded, the group of enemy soldiers stopped firing their weapons. I couldn't see why because I was running. I think they stopped firing because they were running too!

I started carrying three WP grenades after that operation and carried them to my last. Want to break contact? No problem! Toss a white phosphorus grenade. Get in a firefight and want to keep the enemy from coming in close? No problem! Start tossing WP grenades or call for artillery fire that is a mix of high explosive and white phosphorus rounds. I don't care how good a soldier you are. When that blast of white burning hell explodes into a shower of hot glowing metal, your mind says, "Feet, get my ass away from here." You can't shoot straight anymore under those conditions. You stop thinking about where the enemy is or what he is doing. Your only thought becomes, this shit could burn me or is burning me and I want to get away from here.

Viet Nam was a stress test. I learned to see things in a different perspective. In life's daily challenges, if you don't have red and green tracers flying by you it just isn't a major problem. In other words, life and death situations are important.

Illness is important. Most of everything else, comparably, is not critical.

The human animal doesn't really need a whole lot to be happy. It is greed, envy, and the wanting of things we can't afford that usually get us screwed up. And the micromanagement of everything in our lives that consumes most of our time. If you are not likely to remember the situation six weeks from now, the problem just isn't that important, nor is the solution. When I was growing up, I was told to take care of all the little things and the big things will take care of themselves. Wrong. Worry with the major things. Give the little things to others to take care of.

20

WOMEN AND BABY KILLERS

For some reason, when you talk about Vietnam, the subject of atrocities always seems to come up. People want to know about all the rapes and the reasons for cutting off ears, heads, or fingers. During the war the general public came to believe that American soldiers committed atrocities on a daily or weekly basis. Stories of soldiers raping and killing women or children and the burning of homes seemed to abound.

Along with the stories of raping and killing there were tales of soldiers cutting off ears or fingers to prove body counts. I never saw this done! I never knew any veteran who admitted to committing such acts or personally saw such things done. I don't think American soldiers did this. If it did happen it was an isolated event or a very small number of events. What command or commander is going to say "I don't believe the after action reports I'm getting. Send me some fingers or ears to prove your figures". Doing so would end any military career.

With all of the cameras that were in country, there was no need to cut off body parts to prove body counts. Then there is the question of "who would you turn the fingers or ears into?" I've never talked to anyone who saw fingers or ears being counted. Nor have I ever had any soldier tell me that he was a finger or ear counter. The CIA may have paid for ears or fingers. But no regular military unit would do such a thing.

Yes, there was a place called My Lai. And one company of American soldiers, led by a defective frustrated lieutenant, smeared the good name of thousands of other American soldiers. However, My Lai was the exception and not the rule. The vast majority of American soldiers treated the Vietnamese well.

Rumors grow in combat areas. GI's tend to tell tall tales! "Want to be's", men who never fired a rifle in combat or never assigned to a combat role tell even larger tales! I will give you an example of a tall tale told by some old Special Forces soldiers. Want to control a NVA prisoner? It's easy. You take a piece of det cord and wrap two or three wraps around the prisoner's hands. Then you take the cord and wrap two wraps around his neck. On the running or lose end of the det cord you attached a fuse igniter and a non electric blasting cap. You put your finger in the pull ring of the fuse igniter and the prisoner will follow you anywhere. If he yells or runs, you pop the fuse igniter and he doesn't get very far.

That is a story we used to tell to "legs" and joke about the idea among ourselves. I've mentioned it a hundred times over the past thirty years. Did I ever do it? No! Do I know anyone who did? No! It is nothing more than an idea thought up by an old Special Forces demo man. It started out as an idea to control enemy soldiers. I don't think it was ever done.

Stories like this make me wonder about the soldiers and other service men that claimed atrocities and war crimes were committed in Vietnam. Did they see these things or were they repeating rumors? If they committed war crimes, why were they not prosecuted? If they witnessed war crimes and atrocities, why did they not report it? Failure to report a war crime is a crime. There are two conclusions I have to reach. The first is that these people were and are repeating rumors. Or there was a major cover up by all of the military forces in Vietnam. Could a cover up of any size been kept quiet? I don't think so. Had a cover up of a real event been attempted, I think the news broadcasters would have reported it. They reported on everything else!

Were women killed? Yes! Enemy female soldiers manned aircraft batteries. They pulled guard duty. They manned and ran the enemy's communications networks. They maintained the trail networks. They dug tunnels. And they carried arms and attacked American soldiers. So yes, women were killed. They were killed because they were involved in combat situations and because of collateral damage.

Were homes burned? Yes. Many homes and whole villages were burned under the relocation program adopted by the Army and South Vietnamese government. Were these acts a mistake? Many of us in Special Forces thought so. It went against what we were taught in counterinsurgency operations. The acts made the soldiers and the South Vietnamese government villains in the eyes of those they relocated. But the acts were not crimes.

Were some atrocities committed by American soldiers? I am sure some were. War is not pretty or pleasant. Some soldiers get emotionally involved and want revenge. Bad things have happened in all wars. I'm not making excuses for anything that did happen. But I believe any incidents that did happen were few and far between. The point is that American soldiers were not women and baby killers. They were not rapists. They did not earn or deserve the names they were called when they came home from the Vietnam War!

Were atrocities committed by the VC and the NVA? If you call the execution of the educated and the leaders of towns or villages because they did not want to support the VC an atrocity, then the answer is yes. The VC and NVA entered villages during the night and every civilian that was against their being there was killed. But these incidents were not reported by the press or talked about by the anti war population.

If you call the physical torture of prisoners an atrocity, then the VC and NVA are guilty of that too. But then again, that was not something that was very high on the anti war populations radar. I have a few more things to say about the anti war situation, but I'll save it for later on.

One of the greatest things I learned is that people are people and soldiers are soldiers no matter what country they come from or what language they speak. Individuals want to live, prosper, feed their families, and sustain their culture and religious beliefs. We are very lucky to be born in and have the opportunity to live in America. There may be many things wrong with the way we live and our form of government. But it is the best there is. And until something better comes along, I'll be grateful to have been a soldier and be an American.

21

WHAT WENT WRONG

I am not a scholar of the Viet Nam War. In many ways I spent years avoiding the subject. I was a professional soldier and it was not my duty to decide if my government had made bad decisions during those years. Soldiers can't question their leaders or the causes for which they are asked to fight. They follow orders; provided the orders are not illegal. A soldier's life is simple. It hasn't changed much since the Roman Empire. When you take the king's money, you do what the king says. If you don't like what the king says, you find another king.

For almost thirty years, I have listened to newscasters, pundits, and the general public talk about the war we lost in Vietnam. Because of what I know, I have trouble reconciling that statement with the fact that US ground forces won almost every major battle, and firefight, that US forces engaged in.

The US military forces in Viet Nam didn't lose the war. They were never given the mission of winning the war to begin with. The war was not winnable without taking it north into North Vietnam. The mission, as explained to me when I arrived in county in the summer of 1968, was to assist the South Vietnamese forces so that they could stand and hold against the insurgency in the South and the North Vietnamese forces that were pushing south.

Wars are complex. You lose battles due to one or two things going wrong. You lose wars because a multitude of things go wrong. In a war you have to deal with political, psychological, logistical, tactical, resource, monetary, intelligence, social, and command issues along with the results of physical combat. During the years we were engaged in Vietnam, several of these areas or issues became problematic. What hurt the effort the most were the political, tactical, command, and psychological issues. Some of which we could do nothing about because they lie at the feet of the government in Saigon.

Three of our presidents and their cabinets had a chance to undo the Gordian Knot of Vietnam. Did any of them draw their sword and cleave it? No! They all tried to untangle it. To be fair to Kennedy, he may have been assassinated before he could do what he wanted to do with the issues in Southeast Asia.

For all of the death and destruction caused by the NVA and Viet Cong in the 1968 Tet offensive, it was a military failure. They took and held nothing. They lost over forty thousand killed and we lost about 1500 US and 3000 ARVN soldiers. Along with the loss of bodies their supply of arms and munitions in the South was nearly depleted. What they did gain was a psychological victory by planting the seed of doubt that the war could be won. It was a seed that grew in the minds of the news broadcaster and pundits. And worst of all, it was planted in the minds of our governmental leaders. No thanks in part to the news that was reported. The success stories were seldom in the news; but the death of US military personnel was. Yet they (our federal government) failed to bail out, call it quits, or go all out to win the war.

For a period of time in 1968, there was almost nothing coming south. The VC had little to fight with. Then President Johnson halted the bombing in the northern areas of North Viet Nam in March of 1968. Within weeks of this action the amount of supplies moving south along the Ho Chi Minh Trail increased. In the fall of 1968, President Johnson stopped all of the bombing in North Viet Nam. When this was announced, I saw grown men, professional soldiers, swearing and crying at that news. By the first of the year in 1969, tons of supplies were coming south. And where it used to be coming on bicycles and in carts, it was now coming in trucks and track vehicles. By the spring and summer of 1969, T76 tanks were being reported along the trail. The trail network was not the roadway it would become by the end of the war in the 70's but it was changing. Cart tracks became dirt roads. Dirt roads became paved expressways. What was once maintained with shovels and baskets was being improved with road graders and bulldozers.

If you watched the news and listened to the broadcasters in the late 60's and early 70's, you would believe that most of the young soldiers in Viet Nam were peacenik draftees who only wanted to get drunk, smoke pot, and go home. It seemed like every soldier they interviewed for TV news was out of uniform, had a peace sign on his helmet, beads around his neck, and expressed a desire to frag their leaders and then get wasted.

From my viewpoint of twenty four years in the Army, I would estimate that less than 10 percent of the soldiers in Viet Nam used drugs or committed other crimes. The other 90 percent were young soldiers, who served their tour, obeyed the rules and regulations, and accomplished the missions given to them. The blame for the fall of the Republic of South Viet Nam does not lie with the American Soldier, Sailor, or Marine.

If we did not lose that war, then why did the South not survive the assault from the North and from within? I can offer several reasons. The first is that not all soldiers of the South would stand and fight. For whatever reasons, some soldiers broke and ran. I know of no American fighting unit that did that. I think that some South Vietnamese soldiers shared the views of the Liberation Front. They thought their government was corrupt (it was corrupt), the west had too much influence on their county, and they were not willing to die for something they didn't believe in.

There were always constant rumors and talk about the Republic of South Viet Nam (ARVN) units that would not stand and fight. I don't know how many of those rumors or how many of the stories were true. I believe that the majority of ARVN units fought hard and well. I know that they fought hard against over whelming odds after we left them to fight on their own.

I have to balance this with sitting on a hillside along the border area and digesting what I saw. I watched a company of South Vietnamese infantry move towards the positions of an NVA unit that was about a company (80 to 100 men) in size. When the ARVN company was within a thousand yards or so of where we figured the enemy was waiting, the ARVN company turned, walked away, and did not engage that enemy force.

Why this happened, I don't know. Did they know the enemy was there? I don't know. Did they receive orders not to engage the enemy force? I don't know. I know that there were good ARVN units that fought and beat larger NVA/VC units. I also know from what I saw and what I heard, many ARVN commanders did not fight well and or abused the solders they led. I also know that the indigenous forces, led by US leaders, often fought much larger forces and beat them.

My next reason for failure was the corrupt South Vietnamese government. The war in the South was a guerilla war mixed with a conventional war against North Vietnamese units. To fight a guerilla war, you need a base of support. If that base of support increases and the guerillas are not helped by the population, you win. If it shrinks and the guerillas have help, you lose. Government leaders, from the President of the Republic of South Vietnam on down to the local district leader were corrupt. Bribes and kickbacks ruled. The government took land from the poor locals and gave it to already rich families. While Special Forces units were doing all they could to "win the hearts and minds of the South Vietnamese people," regular Army units and South Vietnamese units were burning down villages and moving people into relocation camps.

You can't win the hearts or minds of people by burning their homes and taking them from their ancestral lands. You win by making their lives better and giving them a reason to support the government and a reason to fight the insurgency. Special Forces soldiers understood that. The regular army leaders did not. Having said all that, the fight against the VC in the South was being won. Prior to Tet in 1968, the VC only staged two major attacks. One was against the air base at Bein Hoa and the other was an attack on the base at Pleiku. There was no major rise up of VC forces after Tet in '68. The CIDG and Phoenix programs were eliminating the VC cadre and keeping the VC well underground. The VC was news, but becoming more of a nuisance than threat to the Government in the South. The real threat was the NVA forces that were forever moving southward and living in camps along the Cambodian border.

Then there is the issue of how Special Forces units were used. I believe that many regular Army commanders didn't understand Special Forces and didn't understand how to use them to fight what initially was a guerrilla war. Most field grade officers of the time didn't like Special Forces units and the way they operated. Special Forces soldiers didn't play by the rules.

In the United States, when pitted against regular army units in war games, they put on civilian clothing. The turned road signs around. They slipped into camps and stole things. They told lies! They embarrassed the regular unit commanders. Special Forces soldiers weren't "regular army" and they, the regular army field grade officers, didn't like it. Vietnam was a guerilla war and an unconventional war. They should have used Special Forces more effectively to fight it.

Special Forces were trained and motivated to fight the war as a guerilla war and an unconventional war. And the major army commanders tried to fight it with conventional troops and tactics. Regular army commanders and leaders were trained to fight conventional battles like those in WWII and Korea. They were trained to stop mechanized infantry in the Fulda Gap. They were rigid in structure and tactics. The war in Vietnam was an unconventional war. Fighting an insurgency and unconventional war required fluid movement and a loose command structure. By the time a commander learned to fight in Vietnam, his tour was over and someone else took over. And the training of the new unit leader began all over again.

Another reason for failure is that the government of the South failed to take advantage of a valuable asset. The indigenous people of Viet Nam were an asset used by Special Forces and Special Ops. The Montagnard people and others inhabited the land before the Vietnamese moved in. The government of the South ignored them for the same reasons we mistreated the American Indians. Racial bigotry and a desire to take the land they lived on! They missed what could have been a great asset. They missed because using the indigenous people would have meant treating them as an equal.

    A major reason the war for South Vietnam failed, rests in the fact that the generals were not allowed to fight the war as it should and could have been fought. Targets in North Vietnam, which, in a normal war would be attacked, could not be touched. Materials, support technicians, and equipment poured into North Vietnam from Chinese and Soviet ships and trains. These ships, aircraft, port and rail facilities could not be attacked for fear of killing the Soviet and Chinese advisors and support personnel that were assisting the North Vietnamese government.

    You can't fight a war with no fire zones and free fire zones. Or this rail yard is a target today but can't be attacked tomorrow. You can't fight a war and allow political concerns to override military need. At times American soldiers were attacked and they could not immediately fire back because permission to do so had to be obtained from a province or district leader. Our leaders in Washington didn't have the balls to take the fight to the North were it should have gone; or tell the Soviets and Chinese to butt out or face American missiles. In defense of our government's policy, I must say that it was a time of nuclear weapons proliferation. And there was, among our leaders, a scare of starting World War Three with the Chinese or Russians. Personally, I think they would have backed down and we would have ended up with a second Korea.

    There is another issue from the war that stayed with the Army for many years. The influx of 90 day wonders and shake and bake NCOs hurt the chain of command for many years. A platoon sergeant can deal with a green Second Lieutenant. He can mentor new non commissioned officers. It is difficult, very difficult to deal with both. There were some instant NCOs that did well. Most were mediocre at best. You can't blame these instant leaders because there is more to the making of a good NCO besides a few hours of training and giving them strips.

However, their poor performance caused future commanders to lose their faith and trust in the non commissioned officer corps. And it was unfair to the young green soldiers to provide them with poorly trained and non experienced leadership. This program of instant leaders didn't affect soldiers in Special Forces. But it took almost 15 years to fix the damage it caused in the regular army.

The hardest issue for me is that we were not there for the final outcome. When the war was lost, it was through a massive conventional attack by North Vietnamese units, spearheaded by soviet tanks, which overwhelmed the ARVN forces. It was an attack in which we did nothing to physically support the South. It was an act that I still do not understand. After more than 18 years of support, first with the French and then with the government of the South, in money, arms, and lives, our government allowed the South to be overrun because of a peace treaty agreement with North Vietnam. We didn't lose the war. We pulled out and left our allies hanging. This was an action that has continued to affect our relationship with nations around the world.

We openly trained and equipped the Army of South Vietnam for fifteen years. If the U.S. military failed in Vietnam, it was in not putting enough backbone into the South Vietnamese Army, providing more heavy armor and anti tank weapons, and lacking the vision of seeing a heavy armor force coming south out of North Vietnam; for it was a conventional force, heavy with armor, that defeated South Vietnam's army.

22

SHOULD WE HAVE BEEN THERE?

The first "should we have been there" question should be answered in regards to the war in general. I grew up a military dependent. I spent four years as a teenage dependent riding a bike across most of Germany and much of France. As a soldier I served in Germany, Korea, and Southeast Asia and worked or trained with German, French, English, Korean, and Asian soldiers. I have stood at the Berlin Wall and looked at the guards and boarded up buildings. That wall and the boarded up buildings wasn't to keep the US and German soldiers out, it was to keep a population from another form of government.

Armies don't fight just to protect a nation's borders and sovereignty. They fight for political and economic reasons far more than in defense of the citizenship. Armies are an extension of the governments they fight under. If a president thinks his foreign policy needs some muscle, he sends in the troops or a gun boat. If someone far off is threatening the nation's economic status, he sends in the troops or a navel task force. If he thinks the supply of materials/oil is threatened, he talks and threatens to sends in the Marines. How many wars have we been part of where fighting took place on American soil? All I can think of is 1812, the skirmishes along the Mexican border in the early 1900's and kicking the Japanese forces off the islands around Alaska in WW II.

You can argue the right or wrong of a war or the just or unjust aspects of it all day long. The question boils down to "was the deployment of troops legal"? Did the President have the legal authority under the Constitution to do what he did? If he did, you lose the argument. If you don't like it, vote him or her out of office. The rest is just political crap.

The draft dodgers and the college students called it an unjust war. By what standards did they measure the unjustness of it? They couldn't! There is no standard. You can argue good and bad, just and unjust, or fair and unfair all day long. And you will take your side based on a point of view, a view tainted by your emotions and your personal feelings. Everyone sees things differently. You can't even argue moral or immoral because there are so many differing sets of values and moral standards in our nation.

Some people believe that war for any reason is wrong. There are those that believe that war is only justified in the physical defense of the country. Then there are those that believe that war is all right under certain conditions; but no American soldier's life should be lost fighting for another society or for resources such as oil. Let's not leave out those who believe war is all right as long as too many lives are not lost. How does someone figure out what number of deaths and injuries is too many? And there are those that think all wars are good; good for the economy, good for employment, and good for opportunities. Finally there are the cowards. Too many in our society don't want to get involved. Every year victim's in our country are attacked and bystanders, their fellow citizens, watch and do nothing. "I'm not getting hurt for someone else. I don't have a dog in that fight! I don't have the time to mess with the police and go to court. I just don't want to get involved", are just some of the excuses. Many of these feelings and sentiments were expressed during the war in Vietnam.

There are those who want to handle every problem through diplomatic channels. They believe that every dispute can be solved by sitting down and talking. The problem with that theory is that unless you are talking from a point of strength, the other side doesn't listen. Diplomatic channels only work when there is mutual gain or the one side believe that other side will kick the hell out of them if they don't come to an agreement. Look at the diplomatic mess before WWII; "Peace in our time". Look at our talks with North Vietnam in the early 1970's. Only bombing kept them at the diplomatic table.

Many of the protesters called the war a civil war and proclaimed we shouldn't have been involved. For the sake of argument, let us set aside the police action in Korea and the precedent established there. And I will agree the war was a civil war! However, in most civil wars, the victor does not execute the educated and well to do in the losing society and force millions of people into slave labor and reeducation camps.

Anyone who thought seriously about the war would have had images of the Soviet tanks in Hungary, boarded up buildings in East Berlin and the hundreds of Soviet gulags and slave labor camps. They should have known what was awaiting the people in South Vietnam once the North took over! I also think that our own revolutionary war was a civil war and we would not have won our freedom if it had not been for the French who provided men and materials to Washington's army.

I have heard the argument that the Vietnamese people didn't really care who or what the government was as long as they could grow their rice and raise their kids. We talked of that during card games in our club. There probably were Vietnamese citizens that thought that way. Some probably didn't care what kind of a government they had. However, the citizens that had tasted democracy and capitalism sure didn't think that way. The indigenous people of the central highlands, whose lives were getting better and better, didn't think that way! And most people in the national government, local governments, and the military didn't think that way.

I have to mention the draft dodgers and college kids that raised so much hell. I know they believed they were right. I know they think the war was an unjust one. I know that many of them did not want to go fight a foreign war. However, I think they failed to see the big picture. I also believe that the main motivation of the youth who were crying "peace" was their not wanting to leave college and end up in harms way. In their actions they aided the enemy! Their demonstrations, along with the Veterans for Peace movement, gave hope of victory to a government our soldiers were fighting. Their actions prolonged the war! Their actions strengthened the resolve of the leaders in North Vietnam. Their demonstration and support for ending the war killed American soldiers and eventually led to the deaths of millions of innocent Vietnamese and Cambodians. I think back and I ask myself, "What if we had stayed with South Vietnam and there had remained a North and South Vietnam"? What would Cambodia and Laos be like today? Would there be three democratic countries there? After we pulled out, Vietnam, Cambodia, and Laos became communist countries and the slaughter there was enormous. Millions went to their deaths and millions more spent the rest of their lives in work camps. And I then wonder if we hadn't fought at all, would we today, still be in a contest with the Soviet Union?

So should we have been there and finished the job? Our government, at the time, was following a policy of containment of the spread of communism. The President had the authority to put boots on the ground. We were assisting in the defense of a capitalistic society on the verge of becoming a democratic one. And when our losses are put into perspective, they were not very large (unless you think that an American life is worth more than the lives of someone in another country). So yes, we should have been there and stayed to finish the job.

As to should we have been in Cambodia, the answer again has to be yes. Going into Cambodia was the only way to slow the movement of men and material south and preserve the quasi democratic government in the South.

23

WAS IT WORTH IT?

The most difficult question to answer is was it worth it? To answer that you must ask what was the cost. I have no idea what the cost was in tax dollars. Nor do I know the exact cost in American lives. The figure 58 thousand comes to mind, but I am not sure that is the correct number. And I have no care to look it up. The number is really immaterial. That statement does not mean that I think the loss of life, the loss of any life, is insignificant. Every soldier's death was a ripple across American society. Each loss brought significant pain to family and friends. I say immaterial because governments and military leaders don't make policy or plans based on how many military people may be killed or injured. Or on how many civilians may come to harm. Or how much an operation or war is going to cost. When a government unleashes the dogs of war it is hopefully a benefit for the masses and not the few. It is kind of like the theory of eminent domain; the government will take from and harm a few to benefit the majority.

The war did cost in human lives. There was a cost in lost limbs and eyes. It cost in failed marriages. To hear some, there was a cost in drug addition (which I don't believe). But looking at the big picture, the cost wasn't great. We killed more on our nation's highways during every two year period of the war than were killed in combat during the whole Vietnam War period. At least the loss in soldiers was for a stated cause (you can argue just or not just) which was to maintain a democracy and stem the spread of communism throughout Southeast Asia. The slaughter on our highways was and is senseless and needless.

The cost to me personally was a year out of my life; a short year away from my family. I say short because the time went by so fast. For that year, I gained knowledge about myself. Soldiers volunteered for Vietnam because the duty there was good. There was no busy work. There was no police call or KP duty. You did the training you needed to do to do your job effectively and efficiently. When the job was done, you went and had a cold beer. There were no hassles, no wasted effort. Vietnam was some of the best duty time I experienced while in the Army.

When I left for Vietnam I was a young man in a uniform. When I came home I was a professional soldier. I had earned my CIB (Combat Infantryman's Badge) and other medals. But of more value, I had learned the necessity of training and planning. I understood what real leadership consisted of. For the rest of my military career, I would make sure that "my soldiers" were well trained. What I learned in Vietnam helped me become a Command Sergeant Major. Without that Vietnam experience, I don't think I would have climbed as high or performed as well as I did in my military career.

24

A QUICK HISTORY LESSON

What you have read is what I experienced during a tour in Vietnam. It is my story. It is what I remember and how I feel about the war. It is also the story of many of the Special Forces soldiers who served in Vietnam. I need to voice the fact that today's Special Forces units and soldiers are different from those in the Vietnam days. It isn't a matter of being better or worse; it is that it was very different then. Special Forces, the Green Berets, was still in its infancy. It had grown quickly in size. But it was still developing and fighting the regular army commanders for respect. In many ways it was like a child, a sometimes unruly child, learning to find its way while developing into an adult.

There were differences that separated Special Forces units from the rest of the Army. Draftees filled the ranks in most of the other units in the Army during the early 1960's. The soldiers in Special Forces units were all volunteers. Many of the soldiers in regular army units were teenagers. The soldiers in Special Forces units were older because you had to be a Sergeant or on a promotion list for Sergeant to apply. Many of the senior sergeants, who were instructors in Training Group and senior sergeants on the teams around me, were veterans of WWII and the Korean War. A few had been members of European resistance groups. Most had several trips to Southeast Asia behind them.

While soldiers in regular army units dealt with poor training and instant Non Commissioned Officers (NCOs), in a Special Forces Group there was an abundance of well trained and experienced NCOs. While the rest of the army experienced racial tension, strife, and some drug use, I only knew total professionalism and a dedication of purpose.

The training has always been for conducting insurgency or counter insurgency operations. The basic mission, as it is now, was to go anywhere in the world to advise, train, and equip a guerilla force and to use that force to harass the enemy and disrupt his lines of communication and supply systems. To do that it meant being able and prepared to manage long periods of time "behind the lines" in enemy held territory.

An operational A-Detachment or Team consisted of two officers, two operations sergeants, two weapons sergeants, two communications sergeants, two engineer sergeants, and two medical sergeants. Twelve highly trained and motivated individuals that could be split into two smaller teams if the need arose. Each team, depending on which Special Forces Group they were in, trained and prepared to operate in a specific area of the world. The training was long and intense. Just like it is today.

The day to day activities were different from the activities in the rest of the Army. They had to be. The mission was different. The training was different. The supervision and rank structure was different. Special Forces was the only command I knew of where a soldier could refuse orders and the only thing that happened was an administrative action. The soldier lost his "S" qualifier for his MOS designation and could no longer serve in a Special Forces unit. The relationship between officers and noncommissioned officers was different.

The attitude in Special Forces units was different from the rest of the army. As a sergeant, E-5, in B Company of the 7th Special Forces Group located at Fort Bragg, I sat on the team house steps and watched senior non commissioned officers (E-7 and E-8's) conduct police call. I pulled kitchen police, KP duty, as a sergeant (E-5), with staff sergeants (E-6's) and once with a sergeant first class (E-7). This just didn't happen in the regular army. In the regular army, sergeants stood around and watched privates and specialists do police call. A sergeant in the regular army never pulled KP duty unless it was for punishment reasons.

Then there was the thinking and actions that were different from todays. While training in the United States, team members often carried personal handguns with live ammunition on field training exercises. At the end of a number of Field Training Exercises (FTX), we were told that the scheduled aircraft was not coming to take us home, so get home the best way you can. And so we did. Some rented U-Haul vans, some caught the Greyhound, and others hitch hiked.

Returning from one field training exercise in the White Mountains of New Hampshire, I had to stop on the shoulder of a New York highway because of a flat tire. A state trooper stopped to assist me. I had a Browning .30 caliber machine gun, a couple of AK-47 and M16 rifles in the trunk of my car. My personal car! When the officer stopped to assist me, I expected a hassle from the officer over the automatic weapons. I imagined going to jail until I could prove that the weapons belonged to the Army and they were legally in my care. It didn't happen. He accepted my story and my military ID and let me go with a caution to be careful. Times have changed in many ways!

Thinking of those days, one thing in the military has really changed and that is the use of alcohol. Lunch on post was often a sandwich and a beer at the NCO club. It was not uncommon while on training exercises in the United States to have a couple of quarts of whisky dropped in along with the re-supplies. Field problems often ended with a pig roast and a keg of beer. Even though alcohol seemed to be everywhere, training and exceeding the established standards was serious business. I can't recall ever seeing a fellow Special Forces soldier intoxicated or impaired during duty hours. Nights and weekends were a different story. When it was time to party, it was as intense as the training. There was no doubt about it, partying was serious business too. Today the consumption of alcohol is discouraged. Having a beer at lunch can cause a soldier serious problems.

The training, the deployments, and the partying took its toll in marriages. The phone calls that came during any part of the day or night that sent teams into isolation were hard for some wives to cope with. They never knew if the alert was for real; if their husbands would be home in three days, three months, or a year later. I was told that the divorce rate in Special Forces during the late 1960's was eighty-five percent. I don't know how close that figure is to reality. But I do know that the divorce rate was high enough to attract the attention of the command structure. Soldiers who wanted to extend their tour or volunteering to return to Vietnam had to have a letter from their spouse indicating that it was all right for them to do so.

People are somewhat amazed when told that my wife and two children spent four weeks with me, in the mountains of New Hampshire, while I ran a safe house during a field training exercise. And that their participation was sanctioned and endorsed by the command, or at least by my immediate supervisors. These were things that just didn't happen in regular army units and they don't happen today in Special Forces units. There was a feeling, among us, that some of the rules and regulations that governed the rest of the Army didn't apply to Special Forces. And a sense that commanders in regular army units did not like, much less understand Special Forces.

We were the cause of some of those hard feelings. I remember a group of us playing football in our underwear on one post and the military police had to order us inside our barracks. While in a school at Ft. Belvoir, a Special Forces soldier bit the head off a small snake. He did it in the mess hall, at breakfast time. It was a joke, but it made some soldiers sick and it was not looked upon kindly by the staff at the school. They put him on KP (Kitchen Police duty) that weekend as a form of punishment. He retaliated by putting soap in some of the food. That got him kicked out of the course and sent back to FT Bragg.

At Ft Bragg, the soldier received what amounted to verbal counseling on existing within the rest of the army and then sent back to FT Belvoir with the next class. Members of the class, angry at his being sent back to Bragg for the snake incident, retaliated by using their arson skills and setting fire to several trash dumpsters on Fort Belvoir and putting toilet paper in the cannon the MP's fired at reveille and retreat. It became a feeling of us against them. Thinking back on it, the actions were somewhat childish. They could possibly have been the acts of a spoiled child. But the acts demonstrate the differences in attitude that existed between us and the rest of the military.

Today's Special Forces soldier is well trained and just as dedicated as we were. His equipment is better and so is the support. But more than that, the general officers and people in command now, view and accept special operations and its soldiers in a way that was not seen in those years long ago. There once was a time when the term "special forces" meant the army's green berets. Today, if you hear a story about "special forces", you don't know if the story is about Army Special Forces, Army Rangers, Navy SEALS, Air Force Commandos, Marine Long Range Patrol, or a Delta Team. Today, all of these teams are called "special forces". And they represent the best each branch of the services has to offer.

Although Special Forces did not actually come into being until 1952, you could say their involvement in Vietnam began in or around 1950 when the United States government began its involvement with the French forces fighting the Communist insurgents in Indochina and the creation of North and South Vietnam. A need was seen in the military for soldiers who could fight and train others to fight a communist insurgency.

In June of 1952 the 10th Special Forces Group was activated at Fort Bragg, North Carolina. With the first war time operations conducted that same year in Korea and continuing throughout the remainder of the Korean War. Within a short period of time following the activation of the 10th, it was split into two parts. Part of the group went to Bad Tolz, Germany as the 10th Special Forces Group and the remaining part was named the 77th Special Forces Group. From the 77th, Special Operational Detachments were organized and brought into being as it became necessary to meet operational requirements abroad.

In 1953 the Eisenhower administration provides money and arms to assist the French who are trying to maintain their foothold in French Indochina. In 1954 the French were defeated at Dein Bien Phu and French Indochina was divided into North and South Vietnam by a Geneva Convention.

By 1958 the Special Forces Groups had been organized into the configuration that took us through the Vietnam era. Special Forces companies were broken down into units called C, B, and A detachments. The smallest unit and the one who put boots on the ground were the A-detachments or A-teams. The role of the Special Forces A-team was to carry out any mission assigned to it by the Army. They were trained to infiltrate by air, land, and sea and to conduct operations deep behind enemy lines. The department of defense already had Army Rangers and Marine Force Recon teams that were trained to conduct reconnaissance, raids, and ambushes behind enemy lines. The A-teams differed from these units in that they were trained to remain behind enemy lines in the role of a trainer and advisor to guerrilla or insurgency forces. The Rangers and Marines were trained to penetrate, complete an operation, and return to friendly lines.

In June of 1957, the 1st Special Forces Group was activated on Okinawa. A detachment from the 1st Group trained a platoon of South Vietnamese Army personnel. This platoon, once trained, became the nucleus for the first Vietnamese Special Forces units, the Lac Luong Dac Biet or LLDB. With this training, ground operations and close contact with the enemy begun for the advisors serving there.

From 1954 to 1956 the Viet Minh were forming action committees for the purpose of propaganda and insurgency operations in South Vietnam. In 1955 the Chinese and Soviet Union pledged support and aid to North Vietnam and to the Viet Minh. In late 1959 and through 1960, the number of incidents between the Viet Cong and the South Vietnamese increased. The growing number of incidents was indications the strength of the communist insurgents was growing to a point of becoming a major threat to the government in the South. In 1960 the National Liberation Front or Vietcong come out into the open in South Vietnam.

In September 1961, President Kennedy announced a program to provide additional military and economic aid to South Vietnam. In 1961 and 1962 the 3rd, 5th, 6th, 7th and 8th Special Forces Groups were activated at Fort Bragg. It was at this point that President Kennedy became interested in and an advocate for Special Forces. In the fall of 1961, President Kennedy visited the Special Warfare Center and reviewed the special warfare program. It was also the time that Special Forces teams began working with the ethnic minority groups in the central highlands of South Vietnam. These ethnic fighters were trained in a program that became the Civilian Irregular Defense Groups or CIDG.

The main mission in Vietnam was to win the hearts and minds of these people and persuade them to remain loyal to the government of South Vietnam. And to organize them into defense groups capable of defeating the Viet Cong. Each Special Forces soldier had a South Vietnamese Army (ARVN) counterpart through which operations were planned and conducted. In most areas this arrangement worked well. However, there were instances where the indigenous population did not trust the ARVN soldiers. In cases where the ARVN leadership was poor or lacking, the Special Forces soldiers had to step in and fill the void. This led to situations were the Special Forces found themselves more and more in direct contact with the enemy and less and less standing back and advising.

To counter the gains by the Viet Cong, the Special Forces teams built camps in the hot or contested areas, trained the irregular forces to defend themselves, formed strike forces to fight the Viet Cong, conducted civic action programs to raise the general populations' standard of living, conducted psychological operations, and set up intelligence operations to gather information of enemy movements. From 1961 to 1965, close to one hundred CIDG camps and or development centers were established. These camps and GIDG units became the major work for Special Forces teams. In the eleven years that Special Forces teams operated in South Vietnam, over two hundred base camps were constructed. And if one were to count all of the compounds from which Special Forces operated, the number would come close to two hundred and fifty.

In the fall of 1964 the 5th Special Forces Group became responsible for all Special Forces operations in Vietnam. Prior to this, detachments were formed from within the other groups in Okinawa or Fort Bragg and the detachments were sent to Vietnam to fulfill a mission requirement. After 1964, Special Forces personnel were assigned to the 5th Groups and then on to specific A, B, or C detachment that needed replacements. Some operational detachments did continue to be formed in other groups and come into Vietnam for specific missions of short duration. However, overall control remained with the 5th Special Forces Group.

In 1966 the intelligence gathering ability started to make great gains. Intelligence gathering went from a fragmented effort to a coordinated one. An intelligence program was drawn up that ranged from the efforts in the A-teams to the start of the special projects or special ops. What this accomplished was a much faster and more accurate system for the collection, analysis and evaluation of information, and the dissemination of information on enemy forces and their movements. It also resulted in a breakdown and elimination of the Viet Cong infrastructure. More than half of the intelligence gathered in Vietnam came from these efforts.

In 1970 and 1971 most of the operational compounds were turned over to the LLDB and ARVN Rangers. What wasn't turned over to a Vietnamese unit was dismantled or destroyed and the Special Forces soldiers began to come home. In 1971 the 5th Special Forces Group returned to Fort Bragg.

Although the Special Forces teams of this era were primarily associated with Vietnam, Special Forces teams operated in most of Central and South America during the war years. In Bolivia, Guatemala, Columbia, Venezuela, and the Dominican Republic they completed missions as trainers to the host countries and were involved in counter insurgency operations against communist guerrillas. Teams also conducted civic action programs in the poor rural areas of our own United States. Lastly, while supporting operations all over the world, they continued to train and maintain teams designated for operations in most of the Soviet block countries.

Glossary

A-Camp   A camp or compound under the control of a special forces A-team. These camps were usually in rural areas and along the border areas. They were established to train the local people to defend their homes and fight the Viet Cong.

ARVN   Army of the Republic of Vietnam or The army of the South Vietnamese Government.

B-40   A 40mm rocket launcher. Same as RPG2; a rocket propelled grenade.

BERM   A wall or mound of earth of some linear length. Berms have been used as a defensive work by man for ages. They were used heavily by the Roman army to protect their encampments.

C and C   Command and Control

CCS   Command and Control South. MAC-V SOG's designation for our unit. There was also a CCC (Command and Control Central) and a CCN (Command and Control North).

CHIEU HOI   An NVA soldiers who gave up and agreed to work for the allied forces.

CIDG   Civilian Irregular Defense Group. Paramilitary counterinsurgency companies formed and trained by Special Forces personnel to combat the Viet Cong.

DEMO MAN   The engineer man on a Special Forces team. Special Forces engineers are trained in the making of and use of a wide range of explosives.

DET Cord   A flexible linear explosive (PETN) that resembles plastic closes line.

DUSTER   A tank like track vehicle with twin 40 mm antiaircraft cannons. The system was developed in WWII as an anti aircraft weapon and was used in Vietnam against ground troops.

Exfill   Short for ex-filtration or getting out of an area

FAC   Forward Air Controller. They were the traffic cops in the sky. They marked targets with rockets and directed strike aircraft to their targets.

Frag   A fragmentation grenade. A grenade with a metal body and a filler that explodes. The body breaks up and the flying metal fragments cause injuries and death.

FRENCH TOILET A hole in the floor surrounded by tile which you used by squatting over it.

FTX   Field Training Exercise

Gunship   A helicopter armed with rocket pods and mini guns.

Intel   Short for intelligence. That which is produced after analyzing information, the information gathered for intelligence purposes, or the section of people who turn information into intelligence.

Isolation When a Special Forces team was alerted for a mission they went into isolation. The team was placed in a guarded building with no window. Once there they were given a mission order and issued maps, target folders, equipment, and weapons. The team did not know if the mission they were preparing for was real or if it was just training. Once in isolation, they had no contact with anyone outside of the isolation building until the mission was completed.

Italian Green   Code name given to a variety of booby trapped munitions (61mm mortar rounds, 12.7 mm rounds, and 7.62 X 57 rounds) that would explode on use. It was dropped along trails or "salted" in enemy caches.

Kilometer   One thousand meters or 5/8 of a mile.

Leg   Or "straight leg", a non airborne soldier.

LLDB   Luc Luong Dac Biet. LLDB soldiers (South Vietnamese Special Forces) did not fall under the normal ARVN chain of command. They were special operational units that came under the Vietnamese Presidential Liaison Office

LZ   Landing Zone A clearing in the jungle large enough for one or more helicopters to set down. Any area designated as a landing zone.

MAC-V   Military Assistance Command- Vietnam The command structure which ran the war in Vietnam.

McGUIRE RIG   A sling on the end of a rope that a soldier could sit in, pull around his chest and under his arms, or simply attach to his wrist and be pulled up and out of an area by a helicopter.

Mike Force   A reaction force, often made up of former CIDG members.

Minigun   A Gattling type machine gun with six rotating barrels that could fire 4 to 6 thousand rounds a minute.

MNONG An indigenous tribe of Ethnic Thai that lived in the central highlands.

MONTAGNARD The largest minority group of indigenous people who lived in the central highlands of South Vietnam. The designation consisted of several different groups or tribes.

MOS Military Occupational Specialty. Your job in the Army. It is designated by two numbers and a letter.

NCO Non Commissioned Officer A person of one of the sergeant ranks or a corporal.

NVA A soldier or unit of the Peoples Army of Vietnam, the army of North Vietnam.

NUNGS Indigenous people who lived in the central highlands of Chinese decent

OCS Officers Candidate School

O & I Operations and Intel. A school or course required to obtain the MOS 11F (Operations Sergeant).

One-one The second American on a SOG recon team.

One-zero The senior American or team leader on a SOG recon team. The One-zero was usually the most experience person on a team. If a third American was on a team, he was designated the One-two.

OP-35 – One of several operations sections in MAC-V, SOG. It controlled the operations conducted at CCS, CCC, and CCN.

Ops Short for "operations".

RHADE The principle and largest tribe of Montagnards.

RON Short for "remain over night". The night time position of a team or unit.

RECONDO The recon team leaders school in Vietnam. In September 1966 the 5th SFG established the MAC-V recon school. The school taught long range patrolling skills like immediate action drills for breaking contact, survival, map reading, orienteering, survival techniques, escape and evasion, and insertion techniques. The instructor core came from Delta Project members. Their compound was adjacent to the Recondo School. The school was closed in November 1970.

RUCKSACK A knapsack, a nylon or canvas bag with shoulder straps and worn or carried on the back.

S-2 The intelligence officer or section in a unit below Division level where the designation becomes G-2.

S-3 The operations officer or section in a unit below Division level where the designation becomes G-3.

SAPPER A soldier engineer especially trained in the construction and demolition of field fortifications and the use of explosives and mines.

Slick A helicopter that had a mission of carrying troops and or cargo. They often had an M-60 machine gun mounted on each side of the aircraft that were fired by the crew chief and an assigned door gunner.

SOA Special Operations Augmentation The assignment designation was for personnel assigned from 5th Special Forces Group to MAC-V / SOG.

SOG Studies and Observation Group The name given to units doing classified missions under the control of the Military Assistance Command-Vietnam. SOG team personnel and support came from Special Forces, Navy SEALS, Air

Commando, Army Rangers and Marine Force Recon personnel. Some say SOG stood for Special Operations Group.

SPOOKY A C47 gunship. A C47 with 3 miniguns mounted in the cargo bay. The guns fired through holes or ports cut into the side of the airplane. The airplane would circle an area and saturate the ground below with bullets.

Thermite A mixture of powder aluminum and iron that burns at around 3000 degrees.

VC Viet Cong. The Peoples Liberation Front. The insurgents trying to topple the government of South Vietnam.

Willie peter Short for white phosphorus. The M15 white phosphorus grenade weighed about two pounds and had a bursting radius that was just a little less than 20 meters. White phosphorus was used in grenades, rockets, and artillery rounds as a marking round, screening round, and to start fires.

BIBLIOGRAPHY

Kelly, Francis J. Colonel, Vietnam Studies, "US Army Special Forces 1961-1971, Department of the Army, 1973

About the Author

Walter J. Jackson is the son of Jay and Evalyn Jackson of Fort Walton Beach, Florida. The oldest of four brothers (Bill, Norman and Alan), he was born in Orlando, Florida, in 1944. He graduated from Nurnberg American High in Furth, Germany, in 1963 and entered the US Army in 1965 from Fort Walton Beach, Florida.

His Army career spanned twenty-four years. Jackson served in the 7th, 5th and 10th Special Forces Groups and numerous Engineer Battalions. He served as a Platoon Sergeant, Instructor, Drill Sergeant, Army Recruiter, First Sergeant, and Command Sergeant Major.

His major awards and badges include the Bronze Star Medal, Air Medal, Combat Infantryman's Badge, Vietnam Service Medal, Parachute Badge, Vietnamese Parachute Badge, French Commando Badge, Army Recruiter Badge, Drill Sergeant Badge, and the Meritorious Service Medal. He retired as a Command Sergeant Major.

Married in 1966, he has twin daughters and seven grandchildren.

Jackson is currently a Sergeant in Criminal Investigation Division, Lowndes County Sheriff's Office, Valdosta, Georgia, with duties as a crime scene investigator. He has also published *Soldier's Study Guide* (Stackpole Books).

www.ingramcontent.com/pod-product-compliance
Lightning Source LLC
Chambersburg PA
CBHW071429160426
43195CB00013B/1848